SHAMBHALA DRAGON EDITIONS

The dragon is an age-old symbol of the highest spiritual essence, embodying wisdom, strength, and the divine power of transformation. In this spirit, Shambhala Dragon Editions offers a treasury of readings in the sacred knowledge of Asia. In presenting the works of authors both ancient and modern, we seek to make these teachings accessible to lovers of wisdom everywhere.

This calligraphy features the words *'ishq, 'ashiq, ma'shūq* (love, lover, beloved) and three verses from Rumi's *Mathnawī*.

RUMI'S WORLD

*The Life and Work
of the Great Sufi Poet*

ANNEMARIE SCHIMMEL

SHAMBHALA
Boston & London
2001

Shambhala Publications, Inc.
Horticultural Hall
300 Massachusetts Avenue
Boston, Massachusetts 02115
www.shambhala.com

9 8 7 6 5 4

Printed in the United States of America
⊗This edition is printed on acid-free paper that meets the
American National Standards Institute z39.48 Standard.
♻Shambhala Publications makes every effort to print on recycled paper.
For more information please visit www.shambhala.com.
Distributed in the United States by Random House, Inc.,
and in Canada by Random House of Canada Ltd

The Library of Congress Cataloging-in-Publication Data

Schimmel, Annemarie.
Rumi's world : the life and work of the great
Sufi poet / Annemarie Schimmel.
p. cm.
Originally published: I am wind, you are fire.
1st ed. Boston: Shambhala, 1992.
Includes bibliographical references and index.
ISBN 978-0-87773-611-0 (pb)
1. Jalâl al-Dîn Rûmî, Maulana, 1207–1273—Religion.
I. Schimmel, Annemarie. I am wind, you are fire. II. Title.

PK6482.S34 E5 2001
891'.5511—dc21   00-054767

Contents

The Life and Work
of the *Great Sufi Poet*

1

Pilgrimage to Rumi

Come into my house, beloved—a short while!
Quicken our soul, beloved—a short while!
That from Konya radiate light of Love
To Samarqand and Bukhara a short while!

THUS SINGS MAULANA JALALUDDIN RUMI. His dream that the light
of Love might radiate from Konya to Samarqand and Bukhara "for
a short while" was more than fulfilled. For over seven hundred
years this light has illuminated not only the eastern Islamic world
as far as the borders of Bengal but also increasingly the Western
world, where Maulana Rumi's words were introduced through
translations by German and British orientalists from the beginning
of the nineteenth century.

Let us therefore wander to the place whence that light shines,
to Konya! There, Maulana's mausoleum, known as the Yeşil Türbe,
the Green Dome, beckons to the visitor, its turquoise tiles visible
far beyond the center of the Anatolian town known in ancient
times as Iconium.

I used to travel the road from Ankara to Konya often, and now
whenever I speak of it I think of that Anatolia of the 1950s, before
the boom in building and modernization began; it was a time
when one still felt much closer to Maulana's own age, the
thirteenth century, when every step on the road was so to speak a

step on a spiritual pilgrimage. Every stone, every tree seemed to translate Rumi's message into its own silent language for those who had eyes to see and ears to hear.

In those days one usually traveled the two hundred and sixty kilometers from Ankara to Konya by bus. The road wound up to the hills south of the Turkish capital and divided in two at the hundred-kilometer point, the left fork leading to Akşehir and then to the Taurus Mountains—to the Kilikian Gate that opens toward the eastern Mediterranean—while the right fork headed toward Konya. Between the two roads one could see the large Salt Lake, sometimes glittering like a pool of aquamarine crystals, at other times reflecting the setting sun in unearthly pink hues. Beyond it, in the afternoon one might make out the conic shape of the Hasan Dağ, covered with eternal snow, a symbol of the mountain of joy, which one reaches only by wandering through the salt water of tears shed in long, lonely nights.

The road to Konya led through a series of seemingly empty hilly stretches where the houses were almost indistinguishable from the soil. In the spring new lambs could be seen grazing, dotting the fresh grass like so many tiny white flowers. After a straight passage of some sixty kilometers the last small pass over a range of hills was crossed and one descended to the fertile Konya plain, seat of civilization from time immemorial (excavations at Alaca Höyük have brought to light wall paintings from circa 7000 B.C.E.). Through the haze, two volcanic mountains gradually emerged; they form a border to the south, separating the Konya plains from the area around Beyşehir Lake, site of a beautiful mosque with elegant wooden pillars as well as a Hittite sanctuary featuring a relief of the sun god overlooking a vigorous spring. The people call it Eflatun Pīnarī, "Plato's spring," for Plato, so legend tells us, once resided here and used his magic powers to give central Anatolia its present shape. Were not Platonic ideas alive in Anatolia in the days of Maulana Rumi, whose work itself bears traces of Neoplatonic thought?

At the right hand of the road a caravanserai, Horozlu Han, seemed to be waiting to receive travelers. Much of it lay in ruins, yet it still revealed the basic structure of the rest houses that were erected throughout central Anatolia during the reign of the Seljukids: here were the guest chambers, the places for horses and luggage, and a small prayer site. In winter, when heavy snows deluged the plains, it could happen that a traveling party would be forced to stop at such caravanserais for days—and Rumi aptly compares the world of matter to such a guest house, where the souls long for the first warm days of spring when the snow will melt, the rising sun will release the icicles, the ice will break forth into running, life-bestowing water, and the caravan can proceed on its way home.

Leaving Horozlu Han behind us, we slowly enter the precincts of Konya (or rather, we once did so; alas, the Han has been repaired and the lovely ruins are now enshrined in concrete). A small local cemetery dates back in part to the late thirteenth to fourteenth centuries. Would it not be advisable to stop here for a moment? For Sufism itself was based on the meditation of death, the hour when the soul had to meet its Lord after undergoing interrogation by the two angels Munkar and Nakir in the grave. What soul could restrain a shiver in anticipation of the moment when it will stand before the highest Judge to give account of its acts, its thoughts, its words? Hope for Paradise and its bliss, fear of the awful punishments of Hell as described in the Koran, together moved the believers and spurred them to obedience. Yet the Sufis understood better the believers' real concern: Rabi'a, that pious woman from Basra (who died in 801), taught them to love God not from hope or fear, but for the sake of His eternal Beauty: out of pure love. For does not the Koran say: "He loves them and they love Him" (Sura 5/59)? The lovers of God no longer dreaded death but rather longed for it, for "death is a bridge that leads the lover to the Beloved." What could one desire more than to attain the moment when, freed from the fetters of matter, one would contemplate the eternal Divine Beauty, entering into the presence of that unfathomable Divine Being from which everything comes and to which all returns? "Verily we belong to God, and to Him we are returning" (Sura 2/151).

Standing in the midst of these ancient tombstones, we can almost hear the words with which Rumi consoled his friends during his last illness, in the late fall of 1273:

> If death's a man—let him come close to me
> That I can clasp him tightly to my breast!
> I'll take from him a soul, pure, colorless;
> He'll take from me a colored frock, no more! (D 1326)

The nightingale "Soul," the falcon "Spirit" would return to their eternal home—to the rose garden, to the king's fist.

A mausoleum in the cemetery attracts the visitor's eye by its height: it is the burial place of a Seljukid princess, and its presence conveys something of the culture of Rumi's day. Among his admirers and disciples were high-ranking ladies as well as women of less respectable professions, and though the poet sometimes repeated the traditional deprecating remarks about women and their deficient intellect—an image held in common with the medieval Christian world—yet he was well aware of the happiness of marital life and the joys of human love.

Now the road winds into the center of the town, and suddenly the large mosque stands before us on top of a hill. This simple building erected by Sultan Alaeddin Kaykobad in 1221 can accommodate some four thousand devotees at prayer. Bare of outer adornment, it boasts inside a beautiful prayer niche (*miḥrāb*) with refined inscriptions and arabesques in the turquoise, black, and white tiles typical of Seljukid art, and a high wooden pulpit (*minbar*) for the preacher, made of precious woods with complex geometrical designs. How often might Maulana Rumi have stood here on a Friday noon! Prayer was the center of his life—not the prayer that is performed with lips and limbs only, but a prayer that means true union with the Divine Beloved.

> I have prayed so much that I myself turned into prayer—
> Everyone who sees me begs a prayer from me. (D 903)

This couplet may represent the truest self-portrait of the great mystic.

The mosque was at one time attached to the royal palace, of which only one great vault remains standing today. Several stone reliefs in the museum opposite the palace hill suggest how beautifully the palace gates and walls must have been decorated in Rumi's day: time and again he must have passed by the frieze that shows a unicorn lifting an elephant on its horn. This old Oriental fable served Rumi as a symbol of Love's power: is not Love, strong like a unicorn, able to carry off even the most powerful creature? And he must have seen, and may have admired, the figure of a kneeling angel (a guardian angel, perhaps?) that was found here on the site of the palace.

The great mosque of Konya was always a central gathering place for people in Inner Anatolia. For this reason a casket with the most precious relic of Islam, the hair of the Prophet, was once deposited there in a hollow wall in wartime, to be rediscovered in the 1950s by the museum's director, Mehmet Önder, during the course of repairs. The silken cover of the tiny casket exuded a wonderful fragrance of rose otto and reminded us of the deep veneration Maulana felt for the beloved Prophet, "the caravan leader of the soul, Mustafa," as he calls him in an ecstatic poem in which Love invites the soul to return home to the fields of Divine Glory (*kibriyā*).

Descending from the mosque, we enter a comparatively small square building with a perfectly spherical dome. It is the Karatay Medrese, dedicated to the study of natural sciences by a friend of Maulana's, the minister Jalaluddin Karatay, in 1251. Fine stonework with Arabic inscriptions—mainly of the Most Beautiful Names of

God—surround the gate, but the surprise is complete when we enter the building. The dome shows a most intricate network of many-pointed stars interlinked in mysterious ways with each other, again in the turquoise, white, and black tilework of the time. The eye follows five "Turkish triangles" that at each of the four corners form the transition zone from the square to the round drum of the dome above: they are covered with names of the Prophet of Islam, along with the names of earlier prophets, and of Muhammad's first four successors, the "rightly guided caliphs," in square Kufi characters. The drum bears a Koranic inscription in highly stylized plaited Kufi, and then the visitor's eye tries to untangle the rising network of stars until it reaches the window in the apex. Here, at night, one could see the actual stars above, which in turn were reflected in the small basin beneath the dome: "the metaphor leads to Reality." Thus the dome's fascinating pattern of stars, which can be understood only with the help of higher mathematics, leads to the real stars—just as the parables and metaphors in Rumi's work, which often seem to be strangely intertwined, lead the seeker to the living Reality, which in turn is reflected in the water of the purified heart. No building in Konya, or indeed in any country I know, expresses the character of Rumi's poetry better than this delicate madrasa (theological college), now a museum of faience, home of a collection of Seljukid tiles that were found in the royal palace of Kobadabad, near the Beyşehir Lake.

A neighboring madrasa, some hundred meters away, seems much simpler at first glance. In fact the decor is modest, but its gate astounds the visitor. This structure, called Ince Minareli ("the one with the slender minaret"), was built in 1258, a year that proved so critical for the Islamic world. Under Hulagu the Mongols conquered Baghdad, seat of the Abbasid caliph since 750, killed the last ruler of that dynasty, and thus deprived the Muslim world of what had long been a symbol of unity (even though the caliph had rarely wielded any real power for the past several centuries). The year 1258 seemed to mark the end of the old order and hence—so it is often concluded—the end of classical Islamic culture. Two years earlier, the Mongols had besieged Konya but, as tradition has it, were turned away by Maulana's spiritual power.

The gate of the small madrasa beneath the citadel is decorated with a long, twisted Koranic inscription in flawless cursive style: its is one of the first instances of use of the cursive hand in architectural inscriptions and thus marks the beginning of a new artistic consciousness. The Ince Minareli, its slim minaret destroyed decades ago by lightning, serves now as a museum for Seljukid stonework, and one admires the fragments of inscriptions in plaited and knotted Kufi and the few reliefs that have been retrieved from the ruins of the palace.

Passing by other madrasas and mosques, we wander through the narrow streets until we reach a small open tomb protected only by a grid: here lies Sadruddin Qonawi, stepson and greatest interpreter of Ibn 'Arabi (d. 1240), whose mystical system was to pervade the entire Islamic world and largely colored all later commentaries on Rumi's work. Sadruddin and Maulana were of nearly equal age, and the great philosopher died shortly after the enraptured poet. Their approaches to Sufism and the Divine Reality differed: the one followed the way of Knowledge, or gnosis, the other the way of Love; yet they were friends and respected each other, for both recognized that there are as many ways to God as there are human beings. The goldsmiths' bazaar is almost as attractive now as it was when Maulana walked through it and found his friend, the goldsmith Salahuddin. The carpet dealers and the little embroidery shops remind the visitor of some of Maulana's most beautiful lines: did he not want to weave a saddle cloth from his tears and his heart's blood for the heavenly mount Love, or produce precious red satin from his bloodstained tears to spread it before the feet of the Beloved?

The fragrance of perfumes, the scent of myriad foodstuffs permeates the air, and we recall how Konya was (and still is) known for its superb meat dishes and especially its sweets. So one is hardly surprised to encounter, among the metaphors Rumi uses for Love and for the spiritual experiences, a large vocabulary related to food—for "the raw has to be cooked." As for scent, fragrance (bū), it too is a key word in his poetry: scents remind the soul of something past, of a day of happiness in the presence of somebody one loves, and "fragrance is the share of those who do not see," as Maulana says in an allusion to the Koranic story of Yusuf (Joseph), the fragrance of whose shirt cured his father Jacob's blindness.

A small, simple building in the center of the town attracts us next. It is the maqām, the memorial built to Shams-i Tabriz, the man who transformed Maulana into a poet. It is a place that must be visited, for otherwise Shams would be angry, and the result could be disastrous. . . .

Nearby is the former site of Maulana's house, but no trace of it remains. Therefore we turn to the Yeşil Türbe, the mausoleum itself, where we find Rumi's sarcophagus and the coffins of his father and his immediate successors, in a beautiful hall with two domes. One of the two halls served in former times for the Mevlevi ceremonies that were held Fridays following the noontime prayers. The building was transformed into a museum in 1925, after Ataturk closed all the dervish lodges and prohibited any activities of dervish orders. Only Mehmet Dede, an old dervish, was allowed to remain in his minute cell, and it was a moving moment when he took me in his arms to bless me after I had given a talk on 17 December 1954, at the occasion of the first celebration of Maulana's death anniversary. The dervish cells, which are located on two sides of the small garden, have also been converted into sections of the museum, and the huge old kitchen has been restored. It was here that the novice had to serve for a thousand and one days, beginning with the simplest menial duties. The future Mevlevi dervish would learn the recitation and interpretation of Rumi's Mathnawī and was instructed in music and, most important, in the whirling dance, which requires absolute control over the body. A heavy nail in the floor was placed between the first and second toes of the right foot and kept the disciple in the prescribed position, and every day he would learn to whirl around his axis a few seconds longer until he was able to whirl for a full hour or more. After a thousand and one days he was "cooked" and became a full member of the brotherhood.

Even as a museum the Yeşil Türbe remained a place of pilgrimage for the pious, and there were always men and women from the villages, from the cities of Anatolia, and from Istanbul to visit the place. Scholars, too, came to consult the museum's fine library, with its treasures of medieval manuscripts; but gradually the stream of visitors to the mausoleum-museum evolved into tourists who just wanted to see the place without having any real understanding of the importance of Maulana's role and work for Turkish culture and for the mystical life of Islam.

Next to the mausoleum is a small, fragrant garden where the tombstones of several of the mystic's followers convey a feeling of spiritual peace. An Ottoman mosque stands nearby, overlooking the area.

One can find numerous places in Konya that seem to carry the fragrance of Maulana's presence. We used sometimes to take a brightly painted horse carriage to go out to Meram, the garden area on the hillside where several of the new university buildings are now situated. There one could see the brook on whose bank Maulana would picnic with his disciples; the sound of the water mill and the murmuring of the brook often induced him to whirl around or to recite verses in which the mill and gushing water became symbols of life:

> The heart's like grain, and we are like the mill.
> Say, does the mill know why it whirls around?
> The body's stone; the waters are the thoughts—
> The stone says: "Oh, the water understands!"
> The water says: "No, ask the miller, please—

He sent this water downhill—ask *him* why!"
The miller says: "Bread-eater!—should this cease
To move, say then, what would the baker do? . . ." (D 181)

And Maulana would sing of the flowers and rushes that grew by the banks, whose voices he was able to understand.

Konya, with its old houses (many of which have since been torn down and replaced by ugly, functional apartment buildings), its families, its gardens—that was a world in which Maulana's spirit was still very much alive. There were those who carried on the tradition, who not only recited the *Mathnawī,* played the reed flute, and enjoyed writing calligraphic invocations to Maulana, but were themselves "cooked"—who, in other words, matured spiritually to such a degree that they became exemplary disciples of Maulana, as embodiments of that Divine Love which he radiated in his life and in his work. And the visitor will address Rumi as the poet once addressed his beloved:

Behold, I tried all things, turned everywhere
But never found a friend so dear as you.
I tested every fountain, every grape,
But never tasted wine so sweet as you. . . .

ﺑﯿﺶ 2

The Road to Konya

HOW DID MAULANA JALALUDDIN COME TO KONYA? How did he become Maulana Rumi, "Our Master, the Byzantine" (*Rūm* = Byzantium)?

Afghan and Persian admirers still prefer to call Jalaluddin "Balkhi" because his family lived in Balkh before migrating westward. However, their home was not in the actual city of Balkh, since the mid-eighth century a center of Muslim culture in Khorasan (now Afghanistan). Rather, as the Swiss scholar Fritz Meier has shown, it was in the small town of Wakhsh north of the Oxus that Baha'uddin Walad, Jalaluddin's father, lived and worked as a jurist and preacher with mystical inclinations. He was a man of independent judgment and was known to be endowed with visionary power, though he was never a Sufi in the traditional sense of the word. He had several children, but only Jalaluddin, the son born on 30 September 1207, grew to adulthood and is mentioned by later sources.

Wakhsh, which culturally belonged to the Balkh area, was part of the weakening Ghorid empire that was soon to be attacked by the Khwarizmshah. When Jalaluddin was about five years old his father emigrated to Samarqand, apparently leaving his old mother behind. The city was besieged by the Khwarizmshah, who sought to expand his kingdom over the whole of Transoxiana to the Hindu Kush. One of the stories included in Rumi's discourses, *Fīhi mā fīhi* ("In it is what's in it," i.e., potpourri), tells of this siege and how the strength of one woman's prayer preserved her from the army's evil deeds. In Maulana's later work, Khwarizm, his childhood home, appears as a metaphor for spiritual poverty (*faqr*), that laudable quality of the seeker's heart, and as the home of innumerable beauties.

From Samarqand the family seems to have turned westward, but a precise date and route are not known. As the notes Baha kept of this period end with his journey to Samarqand, the family's movements over the next decade or so are known only from the questionable reports of hagiographers. The oft-repeated story that Baha'-i Walad left Balkh because of his enmity with the famous theologian Fakhruddin Razi is unfounded, although the two did not like each other particularly. The reason may rather have been of a political nature: Sultan Walad, Maulana's son and biographer, explains that "God warned him and told him to leave the country, 'for I shall destroy them' " (VN 190). In fact, as Rumi also tells in *Fīhi mā fīhi,* the Khwarizmshah had refused a request of the Mongols and killed some Mongol merchants. The revenge was terrible: Chingiz Khan unleashed his hordes, and in the course of the next few years the Mongols had overrun all of Iran as far as eastern Anatolia and had also reached northwestern India. Soon (in 1241) they were to appear in eastern Europe and near the Chinese Sea. In 1258 they conquered Baghdad and killed the Abbasid caliph, before being stopped finally by the Egyptian Mamluk army at Ayn Jalut in Syria in 1260.

Whether or not Baha'uddin Walad foresaw the impending danger must remain an open question as long as it has not been ascertained in which year he left his native province: it may have been anytime between 1215 and 1220. The family may have gone on to perform the pilgrimage to Mecca; they settled for some time in Aleppo or Damascus, where young Jalaluddin is said to have studied with certain eminent Arabic scholars. Well versed in classical Arabic poetry, he later wrote a considerable number of pleasant, if not memorable, Arabic verses. The stay in Syria was comparatively short; the family traveled due north to Erzincan, in northeastern Anatolia, and continued southwest to Laranda/Karaman, a medium-sized town in central Anatolia, known for its excellent fruits and especially for its peaches (as Maulana's poetry reveals). Laranda was part of the Seljukid kingdom, where Alaeddin Kaykobad then ruled. Here Jalaluddin's mother, Mu'mine Khatun, died; her simple mausoleum is still visited by devotees today.

Jalaluddin, aged eighteen, married a girl from the group that had come along with them from Khorasan. Here in Laranda, in 1226, his first son was born; he was named Sultan Walad, after his grandfather Baha'uddin Walad. Then the family traveled some one hundred kilometers northwest to the capital, Konya, whose sultan, a lover of art and scholarship, welcomed the numerous refugees from Khorasan who sought shelter in his flourishing kingdom. Baha'uddin Walad, now nearly eighty years old, was appointed to a teaching position in one of the madrasas, and Jalaluddin's second son must have been born around this time (1228 or 1229), for he was given the name 'Ala'uddin (Alaeddin), after Jalaluddin's brother who had died in Laranda. Early in 1231, Baha'-i Walad passed away. His son became his successor and began to teach the traditional theological sciences "and spread out the carpet of preaching and interpretation, and gave luster to legal decision and advice and unfurled the flag of the religious law." The deep impact of this occupation on Jalaluddin is evident from the ease with which he later inserted Koranic quotations and *ḥadīth* (traditions from the Prophet) into his poetry and prose.

Up to this point, the young scholar seems to have shown little if any interest in the mystical tradition. His father was a mystic, but it is difficult to judge whether he followed any of the then-established chains of initiation. Fritz Meier has introduced us to Baha'-i Walad's *Ma'ārif,* a collection of notes, diarylike remarks, and sermons that have shocked most of those who tried to read them, for the kind of mystical experiences that this scholar from

Transoxania displays in his writings is very unusual, and the freedom with which he describes his experiences of spiritual love is astounding. Indeed, he experienced the highest mystical states as utterly sensual, as a veritable consummation of love in God's embrace, and he recognized this loving activity of God, His "being with" everything (*ma'iyyat*) in the life of everything created.

> Go into God's lap, and God takes you to his breast and kisses you and displays Himself that you may not run away from Him but put your whole heart upon Him, day and night. (*Ma'ārif*, p. 28)

Jalaluddin seems to have been quite unaware of his father's secret mystical life. Sultan Walad praised his grandfather solely as "the sultan of the scholars . . . much superior to Fakhr-i Razi and a hundred like Avicenna" (VN 187–88), and compares him— "superior to angels in piety"—to the great jurist Abu Hanifa, but does not dwell upon his mystical experiences. But one year after Baha'uddin's demise, one of his former disciples, Burhanuddin Muhaqqiq, arrived in Konya and, upon discovering that his master had died, began to introduce the young Jalaluddin to the works of his father and those of Sana'i. Sana'i, an eloquent court poet in Ghazna (where he died in 1131), turned to didactic poetry and was the first to use the form of *mathnawī*, rhyming couplets, for the expression of mystical and didactic themes. His *Ḥadīqat al-ḥaqīqa* set the model for all later mystical *mathnawīs*. Traces of his poetical imagery and stories taken from his work can be found in Jalaluddin's verse. At one point Jalaluddin even takes up a line by Sana'i and reworks it into an elegy on the master who had passed away more than a hundred years earlier:

> Said someone: "Oh, Master Sana'i is dead!"
> Woe, such a man's death is no small affair!
> He was no straw that is gone with the wind,
> He was no water that froze in the cold,
> He was no comb that broke in the hair,

He was no grain that is crushed by the earth.
A golden treasure was he in the dust. . . .

(D 1007)

Burhanuddin led his disciple through the whole gamut of mystical exercises as they had been elaborated for the past four centuries among the Sufis, and may well have sent him once or twice to Damascus, where several mystics, including Ibn 'Arabi, the *magister magnus,* then resided. He may even have encountered Shams-i Tabriz for the first time in Syria. But of this nothing can be proved. Jalaluddin must also have studied the works of Sana'i's spiritual successor, 'Attar, whom he allegedly met when the family passed through Nishapur on their journey—though again, this legendary meeting may have been invented by hagiographers for the sake of establishing a tangible relationship between the two great spiritual leaders. Shortly after 1240 Burhanuddin left Konya to settle in Kayseri, the ancient Caesarea, where he died somewhat later. His remains lie in a small mausoleum beneath the majestic Mount Erciyas.

The political situation in Anatolia had worsened during Jalaluddin's years of discipleship. Sultan Alaeddin Kaykobad died in 1236, leaving a weak son as his heir. The Mongols drew closer, reaching Erzincan, Kayseri, and Sivas, and great numbers of refugees from the east entered central Anatolia. Strange mystical bands, Haydaris and others, swarmed through the country, sometimes stirring up the discontented population to rebel against the rulers, and thus facilitated the Mongols' advance. These finally gained the upper hand in the former Seljukid kingdom, and in 1251 a triumvirate of princes—more or less puppets of the Mongols—was appointed. For the last fifteen years of Maulana's life, actual power was almost completely in the hands of shrewd and ambitious ministers, among whom Mu'inuddin Parwana must be mentioned.

During the 1230s and early 1240s, Maulana may have led the normal life of a religious scholar, teaching and meditating; he may have tried to use his influence to help one or another poor person, as his letters indicate he did in later life.

Then, late in October 1244, something unexpected happened. On his way home from his madrasa, Jalaluddin encountered a stranger who put a question to him—a question that made the professor swoon. We do not know its exact wording, but according to the most reliable account the stranger asked him who was greater, Muhammad the Prophet or the Persian mystic Bayezid Bistami; for while Bayezid had claimed Subḥānī—"Glory be to me, how great is my majesty!"—the Prophet had acknowledged in his prayer to the Almighty, "We do not know Thee as it behooves."

There are differing versions of this first encounter between Maulana and the dervish who was called Shamsuddin of Tabriz. Shamsuddin means "Sun of Religion," and for Rumi Shams was a veritable sun, a sun that changed his whole life, ignited him, set him aflame, and consumed him in complete love. Had he ever dreamt of such a sun? One verse says:

> Your dream image was in our breast—
> From ruddy dawn we sensed the sun!
>
> (D 2669)

Jalaluddin and Shams became inseparable; they spent days and days together and according to tradition survived for the space of months without the barest human necessities, transported as they were into the sphere of pure Divine Love.

> Your face is like the sun, O Shamsuddin,
> With which the hearts are wandering like clouds!

One can well understand that neither Rumi's family nor his students were pleased with this development. How could the professor neglect his teaching duties and his family? How could he discuss religious topics with the strange dervish whose pedigree in the mystical chains of initiation nobody really knew? Was this not a major scandal? Nor did the haughty dervish probably bother to endear himself to the citizens of Konya, who in turn thoroughly resented his influence on Maulana. Shams must have sensed that some evil was brewing, and one day he disappeared as mysteriously as he had appeared.

> But suddenly God's jealousy appeared,
> And whispering filled all the mouths around,

says Sultan Walad (VN 42).

Jalaluddin was heartbroken. Torn from his sun, what could he do? And yet at this moment his own transformation began: he turned into a poet, began to listen to music, sang, whirled around, hour after hour. He himself did not know what had happened.

> I was ascetic and intelligent, a striving man.
> My healthy state! Why did you fly away, say, like a bird?
>
> (D 2245)

He knew that he himself was not the author of all these verses: rather he was like the flute, which can sing only when the *hamdam,* "he whose breath is congenial," breathes into it. He tried to send letter after letter to Shams, but the dervish's whereabouts were unknown, and no answer came.

> I wrote a hundred letters, I named a hundred roads—
> You seem to read no letters, you seem to know no road!
>
> (D 2572)

He did not mention Shams' name in his verse but alluded to the sun and conjured up stars and constellations, flowers and trees, snow and ice to point to the transforming power of this Sun whose presence he so missed. One is reminded of 'Attar's description of the Sun, which "warmed the essence of the seeds (*dhariyyāt*) and taught the atoms (*dharrāt*) to be lovers" (*Muṣībatnāma,* p. 155).

Then came good tidings: Shams had been seen in Damascus,

the city that Maulana fondly called *Dimishq-i 'ishq,* "The Damascus of Love" (D 2494). Maulana sent his son Sultan Walad, then about twenty, to escort his lost friend home. Sultan Walad has described his journey to Syria and the effort required to return with Shams, who rode on horseback while the young messenger walked. When they reached Konya, so he tells us, Jalaluddin and Shams fell at each other's feet, "and no one knew who was the lover and who the beloved." This time Jalaluddin insisted that Shams stay in his own house, and married him to a young girl who had been brought up in the family. Again the deep, long conversations began, and again jealousy built up. In particular Maulana's younger son, Alaeddin, regarded Shams as an intruder. In the night of 5 December 1248, as Maulana and his friend were talking, Shams was called to the back door. He stepped outside and never returned. Maulana must have sensed what had happened, but he refused to believe that he had lost his friend:

> Who says that the Eternally Living is dead,
> Who says that yonder Sun of Hope is dead—
> He is the sun's enemy; climbing onto the roof,
> He veiled his eyes and cried: "The sun is dead!"

(D RUB. NO. 534)

Maulana was told that Shams had suddenly left, perhaps for Syria, but in reality the dervish had been murdered with the connivance of Alaeddin. It was rumored that he had been stabbed and thrown into a nearby well and his body later hastily removed and buried. Excavations that were undertaken in the late 1950s, when Shams's *maqām* was repaired, in fact revealed the presence of a large tomb covered with hastily prepared ancient plaster.

Shams never returned; and what was life without the Sun? All nature seemed to participate in Maulana's grief:

> The night wears black to tell us that it mourns

Like the wife who wears a black gown after her husband has
passed into the dust! (D 2130)

Is there anything but blackness left after the sun has set? When
someone claimed to have seen Shams, Maulana responded:

If that man said, "I have seen Shams!"
Then ask him, "Where is the road to Heaven?" (D 2186)

Hoping against all hope, Maulana even journeyed to Syria. But then
"he found him in himself, radiant as the moon."

He said: Since I am he, what need to seek?
I am the same as he, his essence speaks!
Indeed I sought my own self, that is sure,
Fermenting in the vat, just like the must.

Thus Sultan Walad reports his father's thoughts (VN 61). A state of
absolute identification had been attained, and while in earlier
poems Shamsuddin's name gradually appears in the middle of the
poem, now it is taken as the *takhalluṣ,* the pen name with which
Maulana signs the verses inspired by the lost beloved whom he
had finally found in himself. He had already realized earlier that
he could no longer hide Shams's name, and had felt that all of
nature was praising the friend along with him:

Not alone I keep on singing
    Shamsuddin and Shamsuddin,
But the nightingale in gardens
    sings, the partridge on the hills. (D 1081)

Now Shamsuddin's name appears as the very name of the poet,
for how could he claim still to have an identity of his own? He was
consumed in the sun of Love; he had experienced total *fanā,*
annihilation, in the beloved. Hence, the collection of Rumi's poems
is usually called *Dīwān-i Shams-i Tabrīz,* "Divan of Shams of Tabriz."

But who was Shams, and what attracted the two men so to each other? Some anecdotes have survived about the wandering dervish of Tabriz, whose spiritual chain of initiation was difficult to ascertain but who was well known to have visited Sufi masters in Syria, including Ibn 'Arabi, whom he regarded as "a pebble," while Maulana seemed to him a radiant jewel. Notorious for his sharp tongue, his biting wit, and his pride, Shams (as he himself states) prayed to find a single person who could endure his company, "and I was directed to Anatolia." His *Maqālāt,* which contains some of his mystical ideas, allows glimpses into the relation between him and Maulana; he jots down—often in rather incoherent form—stories about Sufi masters or recent events whose background is barely known to the modern reader; it reveals the author's deep love for the Prophet Muhammad as much as his criticism of some of the major figures of Sufi history, such as Hallaj and Bayezid Bistami. Most important, the notes show Shams's infatuation with music and whirling dance.

Maulana, on the other hand, had been prepared for the breakthrough. The long years of study with Burhanuddin had provided both theoretical and practical knowledge on the mystical path; but the last step can come only through divine grace, through some extraordinary event that suddenly opens the gates to the realm of pure spirit, to the vast field of *kibriyā,* Divine Glory, of which Maulana sings so passionately. He felt that Shams was dispensing this influx of grace:

> You are the sun, we are like dew—
> you draw us to the heights! (D LINE 35816)

And the poet's whole existence gives witness to Shams, though his tongue may be silent:

> As I am the Sun's servant, I talk only of the Sun! (D 1621)

Out of this feeling he calls upon Shams in words that ring of blasphemy, for he sees in the friend an almost divine being:

> It is not meet that I should call you *banda* ["servant,"
> human]
> But I am afraid to call you God, *khudā*! (D 2768)

Such verses understandably enraged the people of Konya. But
for Maulana there was no doubt:

> Shamsulhaqq [Sun of Divine Truth], if I see in your clear
> mirror
> Aught but God, I am worse than an infidel! (D 1027)

And he knows his difficult position and yet calls out:

> Whether it be infidelity or Islam, listen:
> You are either the light of God or God, *khudā*! (D 2711)

And he qualified this statement in the lines:

> You are that light which said to Moses:
> I am God, I am God, I am God!
>
> (D 1526)

Thus, Shams is like the Burning Bush through which Moses
heard the Divine Voice, and it is the Divine Voice that sounds in
Maulana's ear when Shams addresses him. He also compares Shams
to Jesus, who displayed "the preeternal Divine Nature (*lāhūt*)
through the human nature (*nāsūt*) (D 2617)—terms of Christian
origin that had been used earlier by the martyr-mystic Hallaj. But
it is important to keep one thing in mind. Maulana saw his friend
as the representative of the "Muhammadan Light" in this world:
Shams is the one who knows the mysteries of the Prophet—that
is why the mystical dance as it is performed to this day by the
dervishes begins with a hymn to the Prophet of Islam that
culminates in praise of Shamsuddin. And the beginning of Sura 93,
"By the Morning Light"—which Maulana quotes frequently—
reminds him of Shams:

When you recite "By the Morning Light," see the sun!

Shams himself felt that he had reached the stage of the Beloved, or rather "the pole of all beloveds"; he was no longer a lover—as other mystics had described themselves—but now, united with the Muhammadan Light, had reached a station that was difficult for anyone but Maulana to comprehend. The entire universe seems to participate in the love of these two men; and the beloved friend's name has such power that anyone who utters it will never see his bones decay (D 1235). And Maulana feels:

> When I sleep in the friend's street,
> The Pleiades are pillow and blanket for me! (D 364)

The relationship between Maulana and Shams was nothing like the traditional love of a mature Sufi for a very young boy in whom he saw Divine Beauty manifested and who thus is a *shāhid,* a living witness to Divine Beauty—indeed, it is revealing that the term *shāhid,* favored by most Persian poets, occurs only rarely in Maulana's work. This was the meeting of two mature men, a friendship that had nothing "romantic" about it, although there are sweet, lyrical verses addressing Shams—rather, this association was timeless, mythical; my students have often compared it to the friendship of Gilgamesh and Enkidu. The beloved's name can be taken as a convenient symbol for the whole of their relationship; the sun, all-beneficent and indispensable for the growth of everything on earth, is also dangerous: if it drew nearer, the whole world would be consumed. However much Maulana may sing of his hope for union or even playfully ask the beloved for a kiss so that he may repay it with another poem, however often he may refer to the peace and tenderness he knows in the friend's presence, yet the aspect of the *tremendum* (*jalāl*), the burning pain that is necessary for spiritual growth, is palpable in many of his verses:

Oh, make me thirsty, do not give me water!
Make me your lover! Carry off my sleep! (D 1751)

Maulana himself never really understood how Love had im-
parted song and music to him, the ascetic scholar and good family
man, how it had transformed him, or rather transfigured him.

And the result is three words only:
I burned, I burned, I burned.

After the revelation of complete identification with Shams,
Maulana entered upon a time of relative calm; now, however, he
needed spiritual company with whom to share his experiences.
One might have expected him to draw closer to Sadruddin Qonawi,
for Sadruddin, Ibn 'Arabi's stepson and foremost commentator
and Maulana's senior by a few years, was one of the leading
spiritual masters in the vicinity. But it seems that despite their
mutual respect Maulana was not attracted to Sadruddin's system-
atization of mystical thought. Rather, he found the new companion
he sought in a quite unexpected place.

The story has often been told how Rumi was walking through
the goldsmiths' bazaar in Konya when the silvery sound of the
goldsmiths' hammers "reached his blessed ear" and transported
him into ecstasy. Miniatures in hagiographical works show the
poet taking the goldsmith Salahuddin Zarkub by the hand to whirl
with him through the streets. This story is certainly true, but one
must not forget that Salahuddin was already an old friend. When
he came to Konya in 1235 he had, like Maulana himself, been a
disciple of Burhanuddin; later he had gone back to his village, had
married and returned to the capital. There he soon became
acquainted with Shams, and the meetings between Maulana and
Shams sometimes took place at his home or his shop. This illiterate,
pious man, thus already an integral part of Rumi's spiritual life,
now suddenly appeared to the master as the faithful mirror that
he desperately needed to find his way back to himself.

He who appeared last year in a red gown
Has now arrived dressed in a brownish cloak . . .
The wine is one; only the vessel's changed—
How sweetly does this wine intoxicate! (D 650)

Maulana now wrote some poems under the goldsmith's name, not as fiery as those devoted to Shams, but tender and warm, and in order to further cement the relationship with the friend, he married his son Sultan Walad to Salahuddin's daughter. Maulana loved his daughter-in-law tenderly, and his letters to her are those of a loving father and caring parent. He also helped to procure a dowry for Salahuddin's second daughter with the help of one of his admirers, the wife of an influential minister. Once more the inhabitants of Konya were shocked. What kind of new affair was this? At least Shamsuddin had been a well-educated man with a profound knowledge of the Koran and the tradition; but this man Salahuddin could not even correctly recite the *Fātiḥa,* the first sura of the Koran! What could the learned professor see in him? Maulana's book of discourses, *Fīhi mā fīhi,* reflects his anger at the reaction of his compatriots: instead of expressing gratitude for the presence of this marvelous spiritual guide in their midst, here they are passing negative judgments; whereas people from distant lands, if they would hear of Salahuddin, would fashion shoes of iron and wear them out just to see such a person!

At some point in those years following the death of his first wife, Maulana remarried. Kira Khatun was of Christian background, and the biographers praise her for her piety and see in her "a second Mary." She bore her husband two children, a boy and a girl, and Maulana celebrated the arrival of these new flowers in the garden "World" with ecstatic songs and dance. During this time—in the early 1250s—Maulana emerged more and more as a teacher, although poetry still poured from his pen. The number of his disciples increased, and he was blamed by some upper-class followers for accepting disciples from all walks of life, including a good number of women. But though he made no distinction between social classes, he always emphasized the necessity of proper behavior, *adab.* The outward forms are necessary: when one plants an apricot kernel without the pith, it will not grow, but with the pith it has a chance to develop. Can one not comprehend a letter from its salutation, and a person from his way of standing and speaking? Maulana's attitude is that of the urban mystic, and he disliked the unruly villagers, who appear in his verse as symbols of the unbridled, formless behavior of the *nafs,* the lower instincts, who riot at the marketplace until the market police superintendent—that is, Intellect—arrives and teaches them to behave. It may be that his way of speaking in verses and his exuberant imagery attracted people who were interested not so much in theoretical Sufism as in the living experience. Some of his followers also attended the lectures of Sadruddin Qonawi in order to penetrate the complicated thought system of Ibn 'Arabi, but Maulana kept away from such scholarly deliberations, so much so that he has been accused of a lack of technicality in the *Mathnawī* and reproached for his failure to present the stages and stations on the path in logical sequence.

Among those who attended Maulana and Sadruddin's lessons—or rather meetings—was Mu'inuddin Parwana, the powerful minister of the country during the years that the *Mathnawī* was composed. The Parwana's name appears in various places in *Fīhi mā fīhi,* and Maulana seems to have liked him, though he sometimes criticizes the minister for his shifting political position and his cooperation with the Mongols. The Parwana regretted that his political involvements—with and against the Mongol occupants of the former Seljukid kingdom—made it impossible for him to devote more time to religious observances. Maulana consoled him in a way typical of his attitude: even outworldly unpleasant activities like warfare and the preparation of defense are useful, just as kindling, dried dung, and straw are necessary to heat the bath. In themselves such things may seem repulsive, but they can be employed as instruments of Divine Grace.

While Maulana was teaching and writing, singing and praying, looking after his family and his students, his disciples began to approach him to compose a mystical *mathnawī* like the books of Sana'i and 'Attar (which they were then studying with him). Maulana's favorite student, Husamuddin Chelebi, son of a good middle-class family in Konya, requested the master to write a didactic poem for the disciples' benefit, and it is said that Maulana responded by reciting the first eighteen verses of the *Mathnawī*, which became known as the Song of the Reed. He tells of the longing of the reed flute for the reed bed from which it has been cut, and how its voice reminds the human hearts of their original home, the Divine Presence.

Scholars once dated the beginning of the *Mathnawī* and Maulana's friendship with Husamuddin at around 1258, the year in which Salahuddin Zarkub died after a prolonged illness. Maulana sang a touching threnody for him, featuring the recurring rhyme *girīsta*, "have wept":

> Gabriel's and the angels' wings turned blue;
> For your sake, saints and prophets have wept. . . . (D 2364)

The goldsmith's funeral turned into a whirling dance, in fulfillment of his own wish, as his son-in-law Sultan Walad relates:

> The master spoke: Now for my funeral
> Bring drums and tambourines and kettledrums
> And bring me dancing to my grave, my friends,
> Intoxicated, joyful, clap your hands! (VN 1112)

But Maulana's relationship with Husamuddin goes back much further, for the young boy had even impressed Shamsuddin by his piety and exemplary behavior. In a poem whose text gives its date as 25 November 1256, the night of a planned Mongol attack on

Konya (D 1839), Husamuddin's name is mentioned, and in a number of other lyrical pieces his name appears openly or hidden, as in the following delightful dancing song, which ends with a play on words:

> The soul of the assembly strides forward step by step to the
> assembly,
> A sun on his forehead, and in his right hand goblet and
> goblet . . . (D 1583)

At the end Maulana turns to Arabic:

> If you are a name—now the name is mixed with the
> named—
> No! the name is like the sheath, and the named one like the
> sword [*husām*].

As Shams had liked Husamuddin, it is natural that Maulana should have preferred him to other disciples, and one wonders whether the poems that feature the repeated address *Ey pisar,* "O son!" or if the variations on Hallaj's Arabic verse—"O you of young age, of tender body" (D 2012 a.o.)—address this young disciple.

The dictation of the *Mathnawī* must have begun about 1256. Following the deaths of both Salahuddin and Husamuddin's wife in 1258, however, a gap of four years occurred. Only in 1262 was the second volume taken up, and Maulana alludes in its first pages to the long period that is required until "blood turns into milk." Husamuddin, who appears in the first story of the *Mathnawi* as the beloved but still somewhat immature and impatient disciple, is invested in the second volume with the rank of the master's *khalīfa,* his spiritual successor. For Maulana he was Zia'ulhaqq, "the sunbeam of Divine Truth," that is, he appears as part and parcel of Shams's spiritual personality and thus could be entrusted with the secrets, as Maulana writes in the *Dīwān:*

> O Husamuddin, write the explanation of the Sultan of Love
> [i.e., Shamsuddin]. (D 738)

In such verses one feels the loving relationship between master and disciple waxing stronger, and yet Husamuddin's request at the beginning of the *Mathnawī* to learn more about Shams is refused by Maulana, who finally silences him with these lines:

> It's better that the friend remain in veils!
> Come, listen to the content of the tales:
> It's better that his mysteries be told
> In other people's stories, tales of old! (M I 141)

These are the key verses of the *Mathnawī*, for in all that follows—which amounts to some twenty-five thousand verses—the name of Shams is never mentioned. Yet at the very end of the work Maulana tells the story of Zulaykha, the lovesick wife of Potiphar, and her longing for the beautiful Yusuf—she who sees Yusuf in everything that appears before her, until his very name is "food for her, and fur on days of cold." This is exactly the state of which Maulana sings in the *Dīwān*:

> O you whose name is the nourishment of my intoxicated
>   soul! (D 2229)

The *Mathnawī* is the story of "the nightingale who is separated from the rose" (M I 1802), and even when Husamuddin is praised (M III 2112) as the one who is intended by all the stories of ancient people, one has to remember that he is but "a ray of the Sun."

Husamuddin is also the disciple who is supposed to understand the deeper meaning of the *Mathnawī*, which is written in a simple, flowing meter with eleven syllables to the hemistich. Dictated over a period of years, the work reflects the various topics that interested Rumi at one time or another. There were months when he pondered theoretical questions; here he tells rather obscene stories as metaphors for the highest experiences, there he turns to lively narration to express the upward movement of everything in creation; now anecdotes and traditions from Islamic history are elaborated, now jokes and folktales appear, and then suddenly his lyricism soars to the very pinnacles of the created universe to break through to a translation of the unspeakable bliss of union with the Divine Beloved. Yet there is a secret order behind this seemingly illogical work, similar to the design of the dome of the Karatay Medrese, where large and small many-pointed stars are connected in mysterious ways. Certain favorite themes appear and reappear in the *Mathnawī*. The imagery is generally not as colorful as that of the earlier poems of the *Dīwān,* for the *Mathnawī* is a book for students, and instead of simply proclaiming his love and its expressions, Rumi has directed his speech toward edification. The work contains the entire wisdom of an unusual and yet exemplary life, the fruit of scholarly and poetical activity, of burning in Divine Love and of being revived. There is not a single verse that is not steeped in experience, and often in suffering. For centuries the work has been interpreted in terms of Ibn 'Arabi's theosophical system, but it is rather like a wondrous tree that has produced strange blossoms and fruits, a tree in which birds of different hues are nesting—until they leave the nest "Word" and fly back to their eternal home.

While dictating the *Mathnawī* to Husamuddin, Maulana continued his teaching and his social activities; his letters clearly demonstrate how he cared for the poor and needy and how he tried to persuade influential friends such as Mu'inuddin Parwana to do something for those in need. Despite invitations to travel to Antalya and other places, he remained in Konya, journeying only once a year to the hot springs in Ilgin.

The work on the *Mathnawī,* however, did not preclude the continuation of lyrical poetry: in several poems he gives his age as sixty (D 1419) or even sixty-two (D 1472). It would be interesting to know more about Maulana's association with Fakhruddin 'Iraqi, a mystical singer who lived for almost twenty-five years in Multan, in the southern Punjab, before returning to the Near East after the death of his own master, Baha'uddin Zakariya (in 1266), who introduced the Suhrawardiyya order on the subcontinent. Fakhruddin must have reached Konya about 1267 or 1268, and Mu'inuddin Parwana had a small residence built for him in Tokat, a lovely, warm town close to the Black Sea. 'Iraqi was certainly in close touch with Sadruddin Qonawi, who like him represented the Ibn 'Arabi school (perhaps Sadruddin himself awakened the newcomer's interest in Ibn 'Arabi's theories). His sweet, singable Persian verses must have moved Rumi too, and one is tempted to hear a soft echo of 'Iraqi's melodies in a few late *ghazals* of Maulana.

Years passed. The political situation in Anatolia did not improve, and Maulana saw various friends and relatives come and go; he did not attend the funeral in 1262 of his second son, Alaeddin, whose role in the death of Shams Maulana knew about (or sensed). His younger children grew up, and his younger son joined the order, while Sultan Walad's children were to continue the family tree. But finally Maulana was exhausted. The physicians could not diagnose the illness that befell him in the fall of 1273. Konya shook with earthquakes, and he joked: "The earth is hungry. Soon it will receive a fat morsel!" Or he consoled his friends by reminding them that death is not separation but liberation for the bird of the soul:

> Don't cry: "Woe, parted!" at my burial—
> For me, this is the time of joyful meeting!
> Don't say "Farewell" when I'm put in the grave—
> It is a curtain for eternal grace! (D 911)

And he told them in full anticipation:

> If wheat grows from my dust, and if it's baked
> as bread—intoxication will increase.
> The dough: intoxicated! and the baker!
> The oven too will sing ecstatic hymns!

When you come to my tomb to visit me
Don't come without a drum to see my grave,
For at God's banquet mourners have no place. . . . (D 683)

Maulana left this world during the evening of 17 December 1273, and everyone in Konya—Christians, Jews, and Muslims alike—attended the funeral, as his son tells:

The people of the city, young and old
Were all lamenting, crying, sighing loud,
The villagers as well as Turks and Greeks,
They tore their shirts from grief for this great man.
"He was our Jesus!"—thus the Christians spoke.
"He was our Moses!" said the Jews of him. . . . (VN 121)

Maulana's cat, who had lamented bitterly when he was on his deathbed and whose meowing he had translated for his friends as an expression of the little animal's yearning for the eternal home, refused food after her master's passing and died a week later. Malika Khatun, Maulana's daughter, buried her close to him, as a sign of the relation he had with all creatures because he was a friend of the Creator.

Indeed, it seems that the enduring power of Maulana's poetical word comes from the fact that for him everything was "charged with the grandeur of God," reflected God's *kibriyā,* His Glory, which according to an extra-Koranic divine word is "God's cloak." Maulana understood the silent language of everything created and knew how to interpret and translate it.

An old Oriental belief teaches that the sun can transform ordinary stones into rubies, provided the stones accept these rays and can patiently endure the long period needed for maturation. Rumi himself had been transformed by the touch of the spiritual Sun, and he in turn was able to transform everything that came close to him, changing stones into gems, copper into gold, bread into soul.

After Maulana Jalaluddin's death, his friend Husamuddin Chelebi took over the leadership of the order; Sultan Walad insisted that his father's wish be fulfilled in this regard. He himself became leader after Husamuddin's death in 1284, and it was he who organized the disciples into a true Sufi order and who established the rules for the mystical dance, the *samā*ʿ. When he died, at eighty-six, in 1312, the Mevlevi order was firmly shaped and in a short while was to become one of the most influential mystical orders in Turkey. Its leader had the right to gird every new Ottoman sultan with the sword. Yet the Mevleviyya never crossed the borders of the Ottoman Empire, however widely Maulana's work was read wherever Persian was understood: shortly before 1500, even Hindu brahmins in Bengal "recited the *Mathnawī*," as an Indian historian reports.

It is fascinating to view Maulana's family as a whole, this line of remarkable men. First there is the theologian and visionary Baha'uddin Walad, whose diaries contain passages like glowing, awe-inspiring boulders, passages whose bizarre sensual imagery expresses an intense love of God. As one studies these works, Baha'-i's influence upon his son becomes increasingly clear. Then comes Jalaluddin, who embodies the majesty and beauty, the strength and the sweetness of a perfected man, a poet who became the unsurpassable interpreter of the loving, suffering, yet infinitely trusting heart; a man who surrendered completely to the power of Love to rise to the unspeakable bliss of annihiliation in the Beloved: For some time he found himself mirrored in the quiet heart of Salahuddin, where he experienced *baqā* ("remaining" in God), and finally he entered the "arch of descent" by lovingly teaching his disciples what he himself had learned in the years of ecstasy and suffering. Jalaluddin thus represents the ideal mystic, whose life forms, as it were, a semicircle of "annihiliation," "remaining" and turning back to the creatures completely permeated by the Divine, and speaking out of the direct experience of absolute Love.

The third in line is Sultan Walad. Nothing of his grandfather's ideas and outspoken "mystical sensuality" (if one can call it thus) seems to be present here: he is the obedient son par excellence, three times fulfilling his father's wish and bowing to his father's friends over his personal interests. It was Sultan Walad who brought Shams back from Damascus in order to unite his father with the friend; it was he who married Salahuddin's daughter as his father wished in order to strengthen the bond between the families, and who in fact accepted his father-in-law as a spiritual guide. Finally, after Maulana's death he handed the leadership of the order to his father's last inspiring friend rather than insist on his right as the firstborn and most beloved son. His destined role was to write down his father's life story, and he boasts that Shams, Salahuddin, and Husamuddin have become widely known thanks to his work. In his own poetry—written in both Persian and Turkish—Sultan Walad has tried to retell stories from the *Mathnawī* and ideas from the *Dīwān-i Shams* in a somewhat simpler and less elevated language, to make them available to those general readers who might not be able directly to follow Maulana's flights into the burning Sun of Reality. One often wonders what kind of person Sultan Walad may have been, just as one wonders about his grandfather. Maulana represents the noblest and finest qualities of both, and it is fair to say that he is barely thinkable without the perhaps subconscious influence of his father's spiritual direction or without his son's loving devotion.

3

Poetical Expression

Where am I, where is poetry?
But that Turk breathes into me: Ho, who are you? (D 1949)

THIS COUPLET, WITH ITS CITATION IN TURKISH, expresses Maulana's attitude toward his own verse: he never fully understood how he had turned into a poet. The deprecative remark in *Fīhi mā fīhi* that he spouts verses for the sake of entertaining his friends, "as if someone were to put his hand into tripe to wash it because his guests want to eat tripe," is certainly surprising, coming as it does from a man who wrote nearly forty thousand verses of lyrical poetry and more than twenty-five thousand lines of didactic verse. But one has to remember that poetry, for many pious Muslims, was something almost immoral. Did not the Koranic verdict in Sura 26/266ff. warn against the poets "who roam through every valley and do not do what they say"? For poetry in pre-Islamic times was connected with magic, and in general dealt often with legally prohibited things such as wine and free love: hence Maulana's condemnation of poetry as a most despicable profession among the people of his native country. Yet from the moment Love carried away Maulana's heart "as a falcon carries away a small bird," he, like so many other mystics, had no choice. And like other mystics of various religious traditions, he knew that the heart's highest experience, the ecstasy, the complete unification with the Divine Beloved, the losing of one's consciousness in the spiritual embrace, could not be expressed in human words and— what is equally important—*must* not be expressed lest the uninitiated misunderstand. His father had tried to speak of the secret of God's overnear proximity in terms that shocked the few who read his diaries.

But the spiritual experience is so strong that it must be expressed, albeit through the poor agency of words, expressed in seemingly meaningless paradoxes that, Maulana felt, were like "dust on the mirror Soul." Yet after the first verses that came from his lips soon flowed an almost limitless stream of poems, born during the sound of music, in the whirling dance into which Love's strong hand had dragged him unawares. But is it not astonishing that the poetry thus born in inspiration was in complete harmony with all the rules of classical Arabo-Persian rhetoric? Not at all. Maulana, like every educated gentleman in the medieval Islamic world, had learned by heart large parts of the Koran and knew an immense number of *ḥadīth* (traditions of the Prophet), so that he could readily insert a Koranic quotation or a *ḥadīth* in every first hemistich of a verse (thus D 2346). And if this was thanks to his training as a theologian, yet beyond theology he had also studied religious and nonreligious prose works in Arabic and Persian and many more works in poetry. His main interest seems first to have been classical Arabic poetry, the powerful *qaṣīdas* of Mutanabbi (d. 965) being his favorite book. It is told that Shams thoroughly disliked this poetry and revealed his aversion to his friend in a strange dream in which Shams was shaking poor old Mutanabbi like a shabby puppet. Still, one finds allusions to and occasional quotations from Mutanabbi in Maulana's verse as well as in *Fīhi mā fīhi,* as in the following closing verse of a *ghazal*:

> Silence your Persian words, I'll talk in Arabic:
> "Our heart is consoled by the wine." (D 2266)

Maulana must have read the great masterpiece of rhetorical

artistry, Hariri's *Maqāmāt*, and he was surely acquainted as well with the *Kitāb al-aghānī*, "The Book of Songs," whose author, Abu'l-Faraj al-Isfahani, records everything concerning those Arabic verses that had been set to music in his time, the tenth century. Most of Maulana's animal stories in the *Mathnawī* are taken from *Kalīlah wa Dimna*, a collection of fables of Indian origin that was introduced into Arabic in the late eighth century and has since inspired storytellers all over the world; but *Kalīlah wa Dimna* is, as Rumi says in the *Mathnawī*, "only the husk," while the true kernel of the stories is to be found in his interpretation of the tales.

There is no doubt that young Jalaluddin had studied the classical Arabic works on Sufism such as Abu Talib al-Makki's *Qūt al-qulūb*, ("The Nourishment of Hearts") and Qushayri's *Risāla*, to this day the handiest treatise on Sufism available. Yet he jokes in the *Mathnawī* that "Noah lived happily for nine hundred years without ever studying the *Qūt* or the *Risāla*." Strangely enough, he does not openly mention the work that provided a major source of inspiration for his Sufi thought and that influenced certain stories as well as his way of argumentation: *Ihyā' 'ulūm ad-dīn* ("The Revivification of the Sciences of Religion") of Abu Hamid al-Ghazzali (d. 1111).

Even more profound is Rumi's indebtedness to classical Persian literature. His verse easily calls upon names of the great lovers of early Persian romances such as Wis and Ramin or Wamiq and 'Adhra; allusions to the famous love story of King Mahmud of Ghazna and his Turkish officer Ayaz do not lack either, and the heroes of Nizami's *Khamsa*, the epical, romantic "Quintet," likewise occupy a special place in his work. Particularly close to his heart is the figure of Majnun, who lost his reason under the overwhelming experience of his love for Layla, with whom he felt, in the end, completely identified. Khusrau, Farhad, and Shirin, another group of famous lovers, appear as well, though these do not figure so prominently. A contemporary of Nizami known primarily for his *qaṣīdas* was Khaqani, whom Maulana admired, apparently for his unsurpassable power of language and imagery, or perhaps for his outspoken religious stance. Rumi sometimes quotes a line by Khaqani either directly or through allusion, although he rarely mentions this master poet by name. He also borrows lines from the other great *qaṣīda* writer, Anwari (d. ca. 1190).

Different is the situation with Sana'i, the mystic of Ghazna, whose work was particularly dear to Maulana's instructor Burhan-uddin Muhaqqiq, so much so that some of his disciples even objected to the constant references to Sana'i, as is mentioned in *Fīhi mā fīhi*. Sana'i's *Ḥadīqat al-ḥaqīqa* ("The Orchard of Truth") had become the model for all later mystical *mathnawīs*. It appears that Maulana was also well acquainted with Sana'i's lyrical and panegyric verse, which is distinguished by its vast rhetorical skill and profound thought; but the somewhat earthy, matter-of-fact style of the *Ḥadīqa* impressed Maulana, and a number of Sana'i's favorite expressions, such as *nardibān* ("ladder") and *barg-i bī bargī* ("the possession of not-possession" or "the leaf of leaflessness") occur frequently in his poetry. Even Sana'i's remark that his dirty jokes are not dirty jokes but instruction found its way into the fifth book of the *Mathnawī* (where one can find a number of such "jokes").

The influence of the second great *mathnawī*-writer, Fariduddin 'Attar, seems to be slightly less prominent, although Maulana certainly knew and appreciated 'Attar's works, especially *Manṭiq uṭ-ṭayr* ("The Birds' Conversation" or, in a more accurate rendering, "The Language of the Birds"). The title is an expression of Koranic origin (Sura 27/16) that Rumi, like his predecessor, uses to refer to the secret language of souls that the mystical guide Sulayman (Solomon) speaks with the soul birds. Having studied all these works and probably a great many other sources that cannot be determined with certainty, Maulana was fully acquainted with the rules of poetry and rhetorical forms, and when inspiration descended he had not the slightest problem in applying, knowingly or unwittingly, all the rules of prosody and rhetorics to his verse.

In the early period he used exclusively the lyrical forms of *ghazal* and *rūbāʿi*. The *ghazal,* the traditional form of love lyric, consists generally of five to twelve lines and employs one single rhyme throughout the whole poem. The rhyme often grows into a *radif,* an overrhyme that consists of a word, several words, or even a full sentence. The repetition of a question such as "Where are you?," an assertion ("It is he . . . it is he . . ."), a statement ("Slow! I'm drunk!"), or a request ("Don't go without me . . . don't go without me!") over seven, ten, and even more lines gives the poem a strong expressiveness. The form is sometimes reminiscent of the refrain in folk songs. If the meter permits, the poem may also be split into smaller units within the hemistich, which rhyme with each other while the main rhyme continues through the whole *ghazal.* In *ghazal* form, which (like all Persian poetry) follows strict metrical rules, Maulana could sing almost everything; a study of the relation between meter and content of his poems would be welcome. The *rubāʿī* quatrain (known in the West through Omar Khayyam's *Rubaʿiyat*) has the form *aaxa*; these short, pithy verses were frequently sung at mystical concerts, as becomes clear from some of Maulana's remarks.

But the enraptured mystic sometimes complains of the fetters of meter and form, and there are verses—probably from the earliest period—in which he simply fills a line with the traditional Arabics catchwords for meters, *fāʿilātun muftaʿilun,* or *fāʿilātun fāʿilātun,* and he may sigh, "This *fāʿilātun muftaʿilun* has killed me," or he says in an Arabic ending:

> My friend and physician fills the cup—leave
> the *fāʿilun muftaʿilun* and *fāʿilātun* and *faʿl*

Elsewhere, he sighs:

> Half a *ghazal* remained unspoken in my mouth
> but alas, I have lost head and foot! (D 2378)

Yet the variety of meters used in the *Dīwān* is amazing. What seems even more astonishing is that many of Rumi's poems, although written in perfectly correct 'arūz (as the traditional metrics are called), can easily be scanned according to stress, and one is often tempted just to clap one's hands and reinterpret the musical rhythm out of which this or that poem might have been born. The *ghazals* sometimes give us insight into the process of inspiration:

> Without your presence the *samā'* [whirling dance] is not
> lawful . . .
> Not a single *ghazal* was said without your presence,
> But in the taste of hearing of your letter (*nāma*)
> Five, six *ghazals* were composed. (D 1760)

This emergence of poetry from the dancing movement accounts also for Maulana's predilection for repetitions and for long anaphoras. A frequently quoted example of his typically strong rhythmical and sound patterns is the following passage from a spring poem, with its repeated long stressed *ā*:

> *Bahār āmad bahār āmad bahār-i mushkbār āmad*
> *ān yār āmad ān yār āmad ān yār-i burd-bār āmad . . .*

> The spring has come, the spring has come, the spring with
> loads of musk has come,
> The friend has come, the friend has come, the burden-
> bearing friend has come. . . .

Even stronger is the sound of this poem:

> *Biyā biyā dildār-i man dildār-i man*
> *dar ā dar ā dar kār-i man dar kār-i man*
> *Tū-ī tū-ī gulzār-i man gulzār-i man,*
> *bi-gū bigū asrār-i man asrār-i man.* (D 1785)

Come, come my beloved, my beloved,

Enter, enter into my work, into my work!

You are, you are my rose garden, my rose garden;

Speak, speak my secrets, my secrets.

In certain cases we know how a particular sensual impression triggered off a first line of a poem, as when someone disturbed Rumi by chatting during a *samā'* meeting:

I heard the nonsense which the enemy said, in my heart

(D 1623)

Another story, which cannot be verified from the poems preserved in the *Dīwān* but has a ring of truth to it, tells how a peddler once passed by Maulana's house with fox skins for sale. His cry in Turkish, *"Tilkü, tilkü!"* ("Fox, fox!"), immediately inspired Maulana to compose a poem beginning with the words

Dil kū? Dil kū?

Where is the heart, where is the heart?

In many poems the first line is provocative, intended to attract the listeners' attention. The poet may refer to a comical story:

A Kurd once lost his donkey . . .

or will ask:

What did you eat? Let me smell!

or will begin by describing a neighbor's ailment, which ultimately turns out to be lovesickness.

To this day it is impossible to establish the exact sequence of Rumi's poems. For the works of Persian poets are always arranged according to the alphabetical order of the rhyme, beginning with *ā* as the rhyming letter, and inside this sequence often according to the meter. Thus, early and late verses stand side by side, and only with the help of some inner criteria (such as favorite expressions or allusions to certain events) may we be able to determine which ones belong to the earlier and which to the later period of Maulana's life. In any event, one can assume that passionate *ghazals* with sometimes bizarre imagery belong to the earliest works, for none of them has the name of Shams as *takhalluṣ* (the poet's pen name inserted in the last verse of a poem). Many have not even a proper final line; others end with *khāmūsh* ("Quiet!"), a smaller number with *bas* ("enough!"). Both words, however, appear also in other, lengthy poems that contain stories or allude to themes told in the *Mathnawī* or in *Fīhi mā fīhi* and are most likely to have been written after 1256. The word *khāmūsh* occurs so frequently that some scholars have even taken it as a kind of pen name for Maulana. It seems, however, that the tendency to admonish oneself to silence when the inspiration flags, or when one feels that one has already talked too much, is a natural part of inspired poetry. As Maulana says:

> Enough, enough! You are not less than the water vendor's
> horse:
> When he has found a customer, he takes the little bell off
> its neck. (D 25)

And when intellect, which acts as the *imām* (prayer leader), has fled before the arrival of Love, the muezzin should also silently come down from the minaret (D 2357), as Rumi says half jokingly.

The early poems never mention Shams-i Tabrizi's name directly, yet allude to him subtly where they refer here and there to the sun or play with astronomical terms. For instance, Rumi mentions no name as he asks:

> Is this the Divine Light? Has it come from near God?
>
> (D 2279)

Then gradually Shams's name begins to appear (a fine example of this period of transition is D 757, when the poet tells how he sought his lost heart at midnight and finally found the poor little thing in a corner, whereupon it called out "Shamsuddin!"). Then, at the point when Maulana has realized his identity with the Beloved, Shams's name appears as the *takhallus* where the poet's name should stand. Maulana mentions his own name, Jalaluddin, at the end of a single *ghazal* only, while his friend's name appears a few lines earlier (D 1196).

A similar development is visible in the case of Salahuddin, whose name first appears in the middle of poems that often still bear Shamsuddin's name as *takhalluṣ*. There are also allusions to the *zarkūb*, the goldsmith, before his actual name is revealed. In the third stage of Maulana's life, an identical development takes place with Husamuddin's name, which first appears in connection with that of Shams. Small allusions in some of Maulana's Persian and Arabic verses also help to establish the order of the poems to a certain, though very modest, extent. Yet a good number of poems seem either to belong to the same time period when the *Mathnawī* was composed or to stem from the period between the completion of the first and the beginning of the second book of the *Mathnawī*, that is, between 1258 and 1262. One also finds poems addressed to people outside the circle of his close friends, threnodies for figures unknown to us, wedding songs for his son, educational *ghazals*, and so on. That shows that Maulana continued to compose lyrical poetry to the very end, and some of his most touching verses about death and resurrection were undoubtedly written during the last months or even weeks of his life.

Maulana sometimes pondered the meaning of poetry. Why did he feel himself impelled to say all these verses?

> I read the lovers' story day and night—
> Now I became a story in my love for you (D 1499)

He is, of course, aware of the source of inspiration:

> Each hair of mine has turned to verse and *ghazal*
>> thanks to your love! (D 2329)

He warns his readers, or rather listeners, to enjoy his verses immediately, for they are "like Egyptian bread that will be stale tomorrow." Sometimes he jokes with the beloved, who has asked him to recite a poem:

> Give me a kiss for every verse! (D 1856)

or, in another poem:

> I said, "Four verses," but he said, "No, something better!"
> All right—but give me first some heady wine! (D 2080)

Sometimes he complains also that, although he does not want to sing,

> When I don't sing a *ghazal* he splits my mouth!

His poetry—so he thinks in moments of high ecstasy—is "food for angels," and when he does not talk, the hungry angel comes and forces him to speak. Yet every mystic knows that these words are merely a weak reflection of Reality, like "the fragrance of heavenly apple trees"; and the word is nothing but a nest for the bird "Meaning." One of the finest comparisons is that of poetry with the scent of Yusuf's shirt:

> The preeternal moon is his face, verse and *ghazal* his
>> scent—
> Scent is the share of him who is not familiar with the sight.
>> (D 468)

In other words, poetry conveys the fragrance of the Beloved to those who are blind, like Jacob, and consoles them with its scent, but it can never convey the fullness of Reality.

"Beacon lights"—that may be another description of words;

and the stories Rumi tells in the *Mathnawī* are like measuring vessels for the grain "Meaning," or "Inner Sense." Maulana knows well that the poet's words come according to the understanding of his listeners, but the words are necessary. A child must read books in school, for the maturing spirit needs metaphors, but once it is fully grown, it no longer needs toys or books.

But Rumi knows also that speech hides as much as it reveals: to speak means to close the window opening onto Reality; and the dust that is stirred up by the movement of the broom "Tongue" settles on the mirror "Experience." Hence the constant reminder to be silent:

> Whether you are Arab or Greek or Turk—
> Learn the tongue without tongues! (D 1183)

And when the poet seeks his heart, he is admonished to be silent:

> I called out: "Where does the intoxicated heart go?"
> The king of kings said: "Quiet! It is going toward us!"
>
> (D 898)

Maulana repeated time and again:

> Without your word the soul has no ear,
> Without·your ear the soul has no tongue . . . (D 697)

and in the *Mathnawī* he confesses:

> I think of rhymes, but my beloved says:
> "Don't think of anything but of my face!"

The absolute union with the mystical beloved, which is the basis of so many poems has been expressed in a charming *ghazal*.

> When I seek peace, he is
> the kindly intercessor,
> And when I go to war,

the dagger, that is he;
And when I come to meetings,
   he is the wine and sweetmeat.
And when I come to gardens,
   the fragrance, that is he.
When I go to the mines, deep,
   he is the ruby there,
When I delve in the ocean,
   the precious pearl is he.
When I come to the desert,
   he is a garden there.
When I go to the heaven,
   the brilliant star is he . . .
And when I write a letter
   to my beloved friends,
The paper and the inkwell,
   the ink, the pen is he.
And when I write a poem
   and seek a rhyming word—
The one who spreads the rhymes out
   within my thought, is he! (D 2251)

Rumi's *ghazals* are formally and technically correct, but because they were born out of living and often overwhelming experience, they are different in style from the refined, diamondlike *ghazals* of poets like Hafiz or Jami. Hence they contain words and ideas that one rarely finds anywhere else. Rumi plays sometimes with Greek and Turkish vocabulary, and does not hesitate to address his friend in a Greek *radīf* as *agapos,* "beloved" (D 2542), or insert little Turkish dialogues into his *ghazals.* His use of Arabic, both in isolated instances and in whole lines or even entire poems, is remarkable.

There are lines of frightening cruelty, such as the following, with its remarkably hard alliterative effect:

Kūh kun az kullahā . . .

Make a mountain of skulls, make an ocean from our
> blood . . . (D 1304)

Indeed, the subconscious memory of Shams's blood on his door-step may be reflected in such lines or in the expressed wish to drink blood from the dogs' vessels, "to sit with the dogs at the door of fidelity" (D 2102).

These verses do not reach the cruelty of later Persian poetry but are much more heartfelt than the highly sophisticated descriptions of tortures offered by poets of the postmedieval period. And who but Rumi would have seen the beloved as a trader in hearts, livers, and guts? These grotesque images and comparisons are further served by his outspoken tendency toward the personification of abstracts. Even though Persian and Persianate poetry creates a whole universe of mysterious interconnections, by metaphors become truth—the rose *is* the beloved's cheek, the narcissus *is* an eye—yet, in Maulana's verse one finds an abundance of images that borders on the mythical. Suffice it to mention his numerous verses about poor Sleep, who, mistreated by Love's fists, runs off, or is drowned in an ocean of tears when he wants to enter the lover's eyes; or the numerous descriptions of the heart; or in particular the metaphors for Love, which appears to the poet in every possible form, as king and as thief, as ocean and as fire, as mother and as lion.

Sometimes Maulana finds unusual rhymes or devices, such as a poem featuring a string of deprecating diminutives, in which the ending -*k* is put everywhere (D 2772 is a fine example), and the "shabby little philosopher," *faylasūfak,* or the "ghastly old hag 'World,'" *kampīrak,* appears more than once. He uses puns frequently and takes an oath:

> By the panther (*palang*) of your glory,
> by the crocodile (*nihang*) of your jealousy,
> by the hedgehog (*khadang*) of your glance, (D 772)

and he complains (or boasts, perhaps?) that

> in our palms was wine (*bāda*) and in our head was wind
> (*bād*). (D 7723)

Unusual comparative forms appear frequently: the beloved is addressed as "more gazelle than a gazelle, more moon than the real moon" (*ahūtarī, qamartarī*), and one feels the absolute ease with which such verses were written, said—or, rather, flowed out of him.

Sometimes Maulana inserts proverbs and folk sayings into his verse, in the manner of many poets. A common proverb about the ostrich (*shuturmurgh* or *devekushu,* "camel bird" in Persian and Turkish respectively) is elaborated into a satire about an unreliable person:

> Ho, master, what a bird are you?
>   Your name? What are you good for?
> You do not fly, you do not graze,
>   you little sugar birdie!
> You're like an ostrich. When one says,
>   "Now fly!" then you will say,
> "I am a camel, Arab!—When
>   did camels ever fly?"
> And comes the time to carry loads,
>   you say, "No, I'm a bird!
> When did one burden birds? Oh please,
>   leave this annoying talk!" (D 2622)

One can also find hidden allusions to tradition or folklore. The verse

> How should I worry about the sting of the scorpion, O moon,
>
> For I am drowned in honey like a bee? (D 1015)

sounds perfectly clear with its juxtaposition of two stinging creatures. A fuller reading, however, lies in the folk tradition that the position of the moon in Scorpio is most unfortunate for any undertaking—yet the lover has left this sphere entirely and enjoys the sweetness of union. There is a further allusion: the friend's face is a moon, his curls are scorpions, as many Persian poets claim.

Not only numerous allusions, but even full poems call upon the images of chess and backgammon, with dramatic descriptions of a game with the beloved during the night (D 1558). To decipher such verses properly one needs a solid knowledge of backgammon technique, just as a knowledge of alchemical processes and medicine is necessary for a thorough understanding of Rumi's (and indeed all Persian) poetry.

Sometimes Rumi speaks of actual visions, visions of the ocean of Being out of which figures and bodies rise like foam and billows; sometimes he sees *faqr,* spiritual poverty, as a radiant ruby that confers upon him a ruby-red robe of honor. The visionary account of the Mongol siege of Konya on 25 November 1256 is as remarkable as the long description of Daquqi's experience in the *Mathnawī,* with its changing figures of seven candles, seven human beings, and seven trees.

Rumi finds his images everywhere. He sees the gypsies ropedancing in the streets of Konya and likens his heart to such a gypsy; he transforms the activities of ragpickers and police officers into the acts of Love personified, and confiscation and laundering into symbols of spiritual states. It is this close relation between earthly imagery and the spiritual realities behind it that makes his poetry so unique. One should not expect logical development of imagery, neither in the *Dīwñ* nor in the *Mathnawī,* for the poet is carried away by associations, although sometimes whole stories unfold from a single initial remark in the *Dīwān*. In numerous *ghazals* one can feel how, after a strong, ear-catching initial line, the poet holds on more or less to the sheer thread of rhyme and rhythm, often adding verses that cannot match the poem's strong beginning. Then he may joke that his poem has become too long:

> because I mentioned a camel in the first line, and, after all, a
> camel *is* long. (D 1828)

Or he says that he would like to sing another fifty verses but is afraid lest his beloved be fed up with his words. Often, the end line seems to be absolutely unconnected with the beginning. One of the longest *ghazals* begins with a sad complaint about the autumnal misery in the world, yet the poet soon reverses this negative attitude as he directs his thoughts to the day when spring will reappear. In other *ghazals,* however—especially the great spring odes—the imagery is consistent.

His poetry is like a flame that rises, changes color, sinks back, rises again. Even in the *Mathnawī,* which is meant to serve as a spiritual guide, one cannot detect the same logical structure as in the *mathnawīs* of 'Attar, where the stories are rather clearly separated from one another. Here, this story grows out of that tale, the tale turns into a mystical teaching or, sparked off by a word, a sound, turns into another story; the text sometimes reaches the heights of great poetry, yet on the whole is less "poetical"—but also less paradoxical—than the earlier part of the *Dīwān*. The *Mathnawī,* so Rumi says, is the "shop of Unity," and if he were to say all he had to say, forty camels would not be able to carry it. The *Mathnawī,* swathed as it is in commentaries composed in almost all the languages of the Muslim East, is in a certain way easier to comprehend and appreciate than the *Dīwān,* the poetical expression of an overwhelming experience. The power of the expression, as it seems, sometimes almost scared the poet himself; he was even afraid lest he hurt the friend's feelings:

If my talk be not fitting for your lips,
Take a heavy stone and break my mouth!
When an infant babbles nonsense, does not the kind mother
Put a needle into his lip to teach him? (D 2083)

But whatever the expression was, Maulana knew that he could only speak when he was touched, like a flute, by the breath of the beloved, which made him eloquent; and yet poetry remained a veil, so that he admonishes himself at the close of one *ghazal*:

Leave the *ghazal*—look into *azal,* pre-eternity! (D 2115)

4

A Spring Day in Konya

IN 1903, AN ENGLISH VERSE translation from German of Friedrich Rückert's masterful German poetical version of twenty-four of Maulana's *ghazals* was published by William Hastie, a Scottish clergyman, under the title *The Festival of Spring*. No better name could have been chosen to highlight one of the central themes of Maulana's poetry, the praise of spring—that time when the sun, the focal point of his thoughts, enters the sign of Aries and the world is granted new life. Anyone who has read at least a few of the spring poems in the *Dīwān-i kabīr* (good examples are nos. 871 and 1121) will agree that the poet expresses his feelings here in the clearest language possible and in rapturous form. Still, I believe that only those who have experienced a spring day in Konya can understand how close to reality his images are. Here, after a night's thunderstorm, suddenly the roses open, the city is enveloped in a fragrant veil of fresh green, and the heavy scent of the *iğde* (a willowlike tree with tiny yellow blossoms) perfumes the street. The fields that surrounded the town in former times are filled with hazelnut bushes; soon, poppies, mint, fenugreek, and other herbs will burst forth beside the brooklets that run down the hilly slopes of Meram.

> The rose garden and the sweet basil, all kinds of anemones,
> A violet bed on the dust, and wind and water and fire, O
>   heart!

All of nature, the four elements of the created world, participate in the festival of spring, and the entire countryside turns into a veritable paradise: the earth is filled with the water of the heavenly fountain, Kauthar, and the cypress joyously drinks of it.

We know that Maulana's favorite disciple, Husamuddin Chelebi, owned a garden outside the city, and one can well imagine the master walking or riding out to spend time with his friends in the garden when the air became warm. Tiny black ants would appear on the earth: the first messengers of spring, they were leaving the dark matter, the dust, which does not know the meaning of spring and of life. Maulana may also have seen the tiny worms that live inside the dark prison of trees, unaware of the world outside, unaware that in a few days the dry branch will turn into a paradise of blossoms—for the worm that could imagine such a strange transformation would not be a worm but "reason in a worm's shape," as Maulana says in *Fīhi mā fīhi*.

Winter in the Anatolian highlands can be long and bitterly cold, with snow piled to the rooftops of the low houses and icicles hanging like lacework from the roofs. Those who are deprived of the light and warmth of the Sun, who sit in the shadow, are like ice and snow—deplorable, matter-bound creatures; but they, too, long to be released, to return to water, their original element, even as the isolated human heart yearns to return to the Divine Ocean.

> The snow says all the time: "I'll melt, become a torrent,
> I'll roll toward the sea, for I'm part of the ocean!
> I was alone, was hard, I was congealed and frozen,
> And by affliction's teeth was chewed just like the ice!"
>
> (D 1033)

Still, in the last book of the *Mathnawī* (VI 90), Maulana calls upon Husamuddin, "the Sword of Religion," to wield the sword of the sun to rescue the earth from its icy shroud.

Is not the whole world of matter like ice that will melt on

Doomsday? For spring can be conceived of as a "smaller resurrection"—an image that is in perfect harmony with the Koranic proofs for the day "when the earth brings forth what it held" (Sura 84/4). The wind may represent the blowing of the angel Israfil's trumpet, and whatever has been hidden under the cover of dust and snow becomes visible again, "and those who have done a mustard seed of good will see it" (Sura 99/7). If people would only realize that this world is frozen, their partial intellect "would behave like a donkey on ice" (D 2784); it would slip and lose its way. For who would imagine that snow and ice could be transformed back into the very water that is their origin? That is precisely how the normal intellect denies the transformation of the world of matter into spirit on the day of resurrection. Yet we need only behold how the snow, as it finally melts and turns into water, can fertilize the earth as a veritable Water of Life, so that flowers and green shoots sprout from the seemingly lifeless soil, which now praises the power of the sun. Maulana even applies the Koranic saying "God will buy your souls" (Sura 9/112) to the transformation of ice into water: He will buy ice (a substance used in the Middle Ages to cool sherbets and other dishes) from the human beings and give them in exchange "a sweet melting" (*Fīhi mā fīhi*). Maulana knows that even the smallest trace of this material life hinders man from the full realization of the union with the Beloved.

> In complete annihilation I said: "O king of kings,
> All images have melted in this fire!"
> He spoke: "Your address is still a remnant of this snow—
> As long as the snow remains, the red rose is hidden!"
>
> (D 1033)

Even a single word in praise of the Beloved or proclaiming that one has attained loving union is still a trace of selfishness. The rose garden of perfect union is closed to the seeker as long as the last vestige of ice, of matter-bound ego-consciousness, has not dissolved.

Similarly, only the advent of spring, the melting of the snow, allows the caravans to leave the dark caravanserai to continue their path: so the soul, freed from the bondage of matter, moves along the road that leads to the Beloved, to its home.

For Maulana, winter, especially the month of December, is "a mad thief from whom plants and trees hide their goods," but as soon as "Constable Spring" arrives, the thief runs away to hide himself. Then, praise be to God, the army of rose gardens and fragrant herbs reigns victorious; the lilies have sharpened their swords and daggers as though they were a veritable Dhu'lfiqar, 'Ali's powerful double-edged sword. It was high time for such a victory, for winter had imprisoned all the lovely buds in its dark dungeon!

However, winter can also be seen as the season of "gathering for the sake of spending." All the riches that the trees have collected in their dark treasurehouses, hidden from winter's covetous eyes, will be spent when spring comes. Thus everyone, including the impatient lover, has to practice "fine patience" (Sura 12/18) throughout the winter months, following the example of the trees, which, like blind Jacob, wait patiently for the day when the spring's fragrant breeze will bring them "the scent of Yusuf's shirt," the aroma of the first buds, which, in their lovely green garments look like messengers from paradise. And the trees' patience is required in order to collect the sap in the roots and to spend it at the right moment, that is, when the sun caresses the twigs.

Winter thus is a *khalwa*, the period when the dervish retires into himself to gather spiritual strength. The trees experience the *barg-i bī-bargī*, as Rumi says with a pun that he probably borrowed from Sana'i: *barg* means "leaf" and also "provision," as the trees, bereft of leaves, *bī barg*, come to gather a special *barg*, provision. Completely concentrated upon their inner treasures, they prepare for spring, when the *khalwa* will be replaced by *jilwa,* the "manifestation" of the glorious secrets God has entrusted to them. (This is not Rumi's wording but that of his foremost modern interpreter, Muhammad Iqbal, who saw in this alternation between *khalwa* and *jilwa* the true secret of human life.)

During winter, the seeds that seemed crushed beneath the dust prepare for their resurrection in spring:

> Onions and leeks and poppies will reveal the secret of
>> winter—
> Some will be fresh [lit. "green-headed"], others have
>> lowered heads like violets! (M V 1801)

If the seed has been patient and good, its fruit will appear on Doomsday as a lovely plant; but he who has planted bitter gourds cannot expect sugar cane to appear in the world to come. The resurrection will reveal the fruits of human actions, nay, even of our thoughts, as though they grew visibly in the fields in early spring.

During winter, the lovely soul-birds disappeared. Only the raven—connected with the graveyard, because a raven once taught Cain how to bury his slain brother, Abel (Sura 5/34)—and the black crow remain. For the crow feels happy in autumn when everything begins to congeal and the nightingale has left the rose garden; then it puts on a fine black dress and struts about proudly, not realizing how repulsive it is:

> If the crow but knew its own ugliness,
> It would melt like snow from grief and pain!

If it only knew . . . ! Through the annihilation of its base qualities, it would be able to fly toward the rose garden that opens in springtime, or would understand the suffering falcon's longing for its master's palace! One might wish the unpleasant bird to be killed, for the time of arrival at the friend's rose garden is for

Rumi "the time when the crow Grief is killed." Yet Maulana never gives up hope: by Divine Grace even the crow, inhabitant of the lowlands of the hibernal world of matter, can be transformed into a falcon—even into the noble white falcon "High Aspiration," *himmat*: miserable creature though it is, it can attain to a lofty spiritual state and behold the manifestation of Divine Glory, once it has shed off its snow-bound characteristics. (Rumi uses here a daring pun on the bird's Persian name, *zāgh,* and the Koranic saying *mā zāgha* [Sura 53/13], "The eye did not rove," a reference to the visionary experience of the Prophet.) Such a transformation, however, is possible only through Divine Grace and Love—and Maulana firmly believes that this Grace, this alchemy of Love, is able to perform such a miracle, as truly it can change an ugly demon into an angel, a cunning thief into a skilled policeman.

In spring, when the crow has disappeared, the real soul-birds will return. There is first of all the nightingale, who sings its melodies of longing for the rose throughout Persian and Turkish poetry and is the finest representative of the soul that endlessly repeats its tale of separation from its beloved. But there is also the stork, *laklak,* a bird that is regarded in Turkey as particularly pious. According to folk tradition it performs the pilgrimage to Mecca every year, is dressed in immaculate white robes, and builds its nest preferably on minarets and mosques. We once saw a flock of hundreds of storks in early March in Maulana's country, between Karaman and Konya; tired from their long journey, they had perched across the fields and the road, and people were overjoyed to see this living sign that spring was not far off:

> The stork "Soul" has arrived: the spring has come!—
> Where are you?
> The world is blossoming with lovely leaves and roses!
>
> (D 2854)

The consonant sound, *laklak,* of the pious bird, as Rumi learned from Sana'i, is its constant attestation to God's greatness: *al-mulk lak, al-'izz lak, al-ḥamd lak* ("Thine is the kingdom, Thine is the glory, Thine is the praise!"). Thus the stork can "cast the fire of *tauḥīd* (the acknowledgment that God is one) into a doubtful heart"—for who can remain unmoved in the presence of a bird who professes again and again that God is the One and Only Ruler?

The stork's arrival coincides approximately with Nauruz, the vernal equinox; then the sun enters the sign of Aries—the sun, which constantly reminded Maulana of Shamsuddin, the "Sun of Religion." For once man has experienced the flames of the spiritual sun, he will never return to the winter of material life: "The sun of the soul, *mihr-i jān,* has no autumnal feast, *mihrijān,*" it is ever the same, for it is beyond all imaginable material suns.

When the sun has moved into Aries, spring, like a prophet, can perform its miracles: miracles by which only prophets such as David are blessed:

> The face of the water that was like iron in winter has
> become, through the wind, coats-of-mail—
> The new spring is perhaps the David of our days, weaving
> coats-of-mail from ice! (D 2120)

The frozen water dissolves into little ringlets that move like a coat-of-mail (an image known to Persian poets of the early eleventh century). As David is connected in Islamic legend with the fabrication of coats-of-mail, it was only natural to ascribe this miracle to him—an association that is all the more convenient as David is the poet and musician among the prophets and thus represents that aspect of spring connected with the chirping of the birds, who, the poets claim, sing "Davidian tunes" or recite the psalms (*zabūr*) of David in the morning.

There are other images, too, for the return of spring. Maulana must have observed the Turkoman tribes who pitched their tents

on the plains around Konya each year during wintertime, sur-
rounded by their dogs, as fierce as Iblis, the Satan; but as soon as
spring set in the Turkomans would leave the neighborhood of the
town for the summer pastures (*yayla*) in the hills. As the term *Turk*
in Persian poetry means everything beautiful and strong, and is in
particular applied to the beloved and, in mystical parlance, to the
inhabitants of Paradise, the return of the Turks to the *yayla* became
an appropriate symbol for the arrival of flowers and leaves on the
trees. The tribal *qishlaq,* the winter quarters, is for Maulana the
winter of the body, but the *yayla* is the realm of spiritual life as
represented in the paradisiacal gardens. (He also speaks at times of
the two dwelling places of the nomads as being "the dark
Hindustan of matter" and the lovely, lucid "Turkestan of the
soul"). Indeed, spring is a messenger from Paradise when "those
dressed in green" (*sabzpūsh*)—that is, houris and angels—arrive
from the blue hall of heaven to dwell among humans in order to
remind them of the eternal spiritual beauty.

Spring also means the arrival of warm rains. We can picture
Maulana walking around the hills overlooking Konya, looking up
at the sky as dark rain clouds gather, "pregnant from the ocean of
Love," until they shed their tears over the waiting plants to grant
the country fertility. How could the garden smile as long as the
cloud does not weep?

> Without the eyes—two clouds—the lightning of the heart:
> The fire of God's threat, how could it be allayed?
> How would the herbage grow of union, sweet to taste?
> How would the fountains all gush forth with water pure?
> How would the rosebed tell its secret to the meadow?
> How would the violet make contracts with jasmine?
> How would the plane tree lift its hands in prayer, say?
> How would the trees' heads toss free in the air of Love?
> How would the blossoms shake their sleeves in days of
>   spring

To shed their lovely coins about the garden wide?
How would the tulip's cheek be red like flames and blood?
How would the rose draw out its gold now from its purse?
How would the nightingale follow the rose's scent?
How would the ringdoves call like seekers, "Where, oh
　　where?"
How would the stork repeat his *laklak* from his soul,
To say: "O Helper high, Thine is the kingdom, Thine!"
How would the dust reveal the secrets of its heart?
How would the sky become a garden full of light?

(M II 1655–64)

The awakening of nature in spring corresponds exactly to human behavior. Smiling happens in proportion to weeping; the smile of the garden is the result of the cloud's weeping; and just as the raindrops can help to produce the garden's beauty, the lover's tears will eventually result in a manifestation of Divine Loving-kindness. Thus the hidden possibilities of the heart will unfold under rain and warm sunshine.

The "rain of mercy" is also connected with the Prophet: the villagers in Anatolia still call rain *rahmet,* "mercy," and the relation between this *rahmet* and the Prophet, who was sent as "mercy for the worlds," *rahmatan li'l-'ālamīn* (Sura 21/107), is often intended when rain clouds appear in Maulana's poetry.

To be sure, such poetic images were known among the Sufis at least since the early tenth century. The Baghdadian mystic Abu'l-Husayn an-Nuri had elaborated them in highly poetical Arabic passages; but in Rumi's verse they gain a new actuality: had he himself not wept like a cloud after the Sun of Tabriz had disappeared?

Hence the profusion of spring songs in Rumi's *Dīwān.* The ancient Greek myth of the marriage of heaven and earth, *hieros gamos,* is known to him, but he spiritualizes it, applying it to his own state:

You are my sky, and I'm the earth, bewildered—
What make you constantly flow from my heart?
I'm soil with parched lips! Bring kindly water
That will bring forth a rose bed from the soil!
How does the earth know what you've sown in its heart?
From you it's pregnant, and you know its burden! (D 3048)

Maulana would go out to Meram on a warm spring day to listen to the sound of the water mill, and like the Turkish folk poets after him he could understand its voice, for he knew that the shrieking voice of the water wheel was an expression of its longing for home. Are not lovers constantly turning like the millstone, lamenting without rest? (M VI 911). On the hillside, even more than in the crowded city, he felt the soft breeze that brings new life to the gardens. The breeze symbolizes the life-bestowing breath of the Beloved, like the *nafas ar-raḥmān,* the "breath of the Merciful," that the Prophet felt coming from Yemen, the home of Uways al-Qarani, the shepherd who embraced Islam without knowing the Prophet. Are not the buds and blossoms like pearls and carnelian, the reddish stone found in Yemen? (D 2222). Touched by a spring breeze, the twigs and branches become intoxicated and are caught up in the great dance that permeates all levels of Creation. Do the little twigs not look as if they were merrily stamping their feet on cruel January's tomb and clapping their hands in mystical dance, led by the plane tree, whose leaves have always been compared to human hands?

The twigs start dancing like repenters [who have recently
    entered the mystical path],
the leaves clap their hands like minstrels. (M IV 3264)

From every corner the voices of birds can be heard; the nightingale, mounting to the pulpit of the trees and announcing that the repulsive shriek of the crow is over, leads the musicians, while the ringdove repeats day after day its call—*Kū kū,* "Where,

where?"—until it finds the way to the beloved. The dance of the flowers and trees is a repetition of that dance performed on the day of the Primordial Covenant, when God addressed not-yet-created humanity with His word: *Alastu bi-rabbikum,* "Am I not your Lord?" (Sura 7/172). Rumi understands this divine address as music that made all creatures come forth in a happy dance; the spring breeze reminds him, and everything created, of the primordial union, and of the moment when all beings first entered the world of existence in a loving dance. Many of us may not be aware of this dance, which begins as soon as "the spring breeze of Love" touches the trees and flowers and they realize the truth of the Koranic word: "After difficulty comes ease!" (Sura 94/5). Yet only those twigs and branches may participate in the dance who are willing to cast off the burden of winter. Other branches, dried-up and sapless, frozen during the cold season, are barred from the dance that permeates the entire universe. On the contrary, the sun, waxing stronger every day, intensifies their dryness so that they receive not life but death from its rays. Severed from its rotten roots, the loveless wood will then be cast into the fire, like the "carrier of firewood," the wife of Abu Lahab, the "Father of the Flame" (Sura 111).

Those who have eyes to see will discern the message of eternity in the spring breeze when it becomes visible in the roses and herbs: invisible waves of roses, hidden in the breeze, required the medium of the earth to reveal themselves to the material human eye, just as a human being's innate qualities must be revealed by his or her actions. The spirit needs matter in order to become visible; thus every leaf is a messenger from the realm of nonexistence, *'adam,* and talks with its long hands and fresh green tongue of the creative power of God.

> The grace is from God, but the bodily people
> do not find grace without the veil "Garden" (M V 2338)

Just as Maulana always emphasizes that one must see the reality behind the veil, the rider behind the dust, so too he knows that the thorn is in reality part of the rose:

> It is all roses, although its outside may look like thorns;
> It is light from the Burning Bush, although it may look like
>   fire! (D 859)

The trees for Maulana are perfect likenesses of the dervishes, slowly advancing, slowly growing until they bear full fruit. Their leaves offer the onlooker an understanding of the roots' character and tell also what nourishment the tree has imbibed. The naked branches resemble ascetics who have but to be touched by the friend's lips, his life-bestowing breath, to become fresh and green: asceticism transformed into love, patience into gratitude. And as the twig is moved and kept in motion by the wind (*bād*) once it has given itself to the movement of the cosmic dance, so the heart should be constantly moved by the recollection (*yād*) of the Beloved.

Maulana views the garden with the eye of love and calls his friends to admire with him the just-opening buds:

> Like cats, each of which has taken her kitten into her
>   mouth—
> Why do you not come to look at the mothers in the
>   garden? (D 2854)

The twigs are mothers, and the white buds and opening blossoms resemble innocent kittens, tenderly watched by the mother cat. Was not the earth pregnant for nine months? Indeed, Rumi tends to see "mothers" everywhere. This attitude is expressed most beautifully in another favorite image, his comparison of trees in spring to the Virgin Mary, who became pregnant by the Holy Spirit. Do not the trees in their youthful beauty and innocence surrender to the Divine Breath as manifested in the breeze, which fertilizes them so that they bring forth beautiful flowers and delicious fruits? The comparison itself is not new, but Maulana vividly reworks the traditional image.

Enlivened by the rain of mercy, the sun of Love and the divine breeze, the trees now engage in prayer. Their prayer is the *Fātiḥa*, the first sura of the Koran:

> "We worship Thee!"—that is the garden's prayer
> > in wintertime.
>
> "We ask Thy help!"—that is its cry then
> > in time of spring.
>
> "We worship Thee"—that means: I come to beg,
> > imploring Thee:
>
> Don't leave me in this sorrow, Lord, make wide
> > the door of joy!
>
> "We ask Thee, Lord, for help"—that is, the fullness
> > of ripe, sweet fruit.
>
> Now break my branches and my twigs—protect me,
> > My Lord, My God!
>
> > > (D 2046)

Maulana walks with us through the gardens and teaches us to admire the work of Spring, that master tailor who stitches lovely gowns of green brocade and brings them forth "from the shop of the Invisible." One of his masterpieces is the tulip's dress with its sun-colored collar and its evening-colored hem. Perhaps the tulip has borrowed its splendor from the Friend's fiery cheeks. Or it may have performed its ablutions in blood, like a true martyr. The jasmine reminds the poet of the separation from his beloved, for this flower's name calls out *yās-i man,* "my despair." The lily praises the beauty of the rose "with a hundred tongues" or manifests the miracle of the White Hand (Sura 20/23 et al.), by which Moses proved his prophetic status. In every corner the violet, wrapped in its dark blue gown, sits like a Sufi, its head "on the knee of meditation," or performs its ritual prayer in permanent genuflection on the green prayer rug of the lawn; it is the flower of the mature believer who, though bent with age, is still green and fragrant. And the rose opens to serve as the perfect likeness of the eternal Beloved: was it not born from a drop of the Prophet's perspiration that fell to earth as he performed his heavenly journey, borne by the mysterious mount Buraq, until he reached the immediate presence of God? Hence the rose carries his sweet fragrance. At the same time it is the flower of divine beauty and grandeur, the full moon that emerges from the crescent, the manifestation of perfect joy. It is the *shahsuwār,* the "princely rider" in the garden, beside whom grass and herbs walk afoot, while the thorns protect the radiant prince. But one may also consider that the *shāhid,* the lovely beloved Rose, smiles only because she remembers how the king himself smiled when looking at her (D 1412). Therefore she smiles "with the whole body" (D 84) as does the lover when thinking of his Beloved or of the eternal rose garden; and the lover will also die "with a smile, like the rose" (D 2943).

But it is not only the noble flowers that will open in a sudden burst of joy when spring arrives. The vegetables in the gardens also partake of the happiness of the warmer season. Of course they are on a lower level of development; they are slow-footed and have a long way before them in their pilgrimage toward the Beloved. Still, they too participate in the upward movement of life. Even the silly gourd, which does not understand why the gardener binds its throat—can it not learn to dance along that very rope by which it is bound?

Now that spring has come, the gardens must be tended carefully. Maulana likens the distribution of the water of Intellect (or Universal Reason) through various channels into human beings to water flowing into a garden, and we should be careful lest we cover the surface of this limpid water with the sticks and straw of useless thoughts. The Eternal Distributor knows exactly how much water is needed, and thus he inspires also the teacher's speech according to the capacity of his listeners' minds.

In fact, our thoughts and acts themselves are like a garden, as Maulana explains in *Fīhi mā fīhi* (chap. 55):

> If someone speaks well of another person, the good word returns to him and in reality this praise is for himself. It is like someone who plants a rose bed and odoriferous herbs around his house; whenever he looks out, he sees roses and odoriferous herbs, so that he is constantly in Paradise. When one speaks well of a person, that person becomes one's friend; when one thinks of him, one thinks of a dear friend, and to think of a dear friend is like roses and rose garden, fragrance and repose. But when he speaks ill of someone, that person appears hateful to him; when he thinks of him, . . . his image appears before him as if a scorpion, a thorn, or a thistle had appeared before his eyes.
>
> Now, if you can see by day and night alike roses and rose gardens and the meadows of Iram (Sura 89/4), why do you walk about among thorn bushes and snakes?

In the gardens of Konya the bees are beginning to swarm again, preparing their wax and honey; were they not singled out in the Koran (Sura 16/70) as signs of God's inspiration? They resemble the perfect saint who provides the world with sweetness and light. (And the honey they prepare, as Rumi makes us understand, is always "licked"—even kings lick the honey of spiritual grace.)

Now the birds start laying their eggs, wherein the white and the yolk are separated by a fine skin, like the *barzakh* that separates heaven and hell. But once the egg (symbol of the human being or even the entire creation) is hatched under the wings of God's grace and the full-fledged bird is produced, the former division of white and yellow is no longer visible. Soon there will be young pigeons in the pigeon houses, and the lover addresses his beloved:

> We are the baby pigeons in your cote,
> We circumambulate your portico. (D 1673)

For how should the pigeon, nourished as it is by the beloved's hand, fly to any other place? With fluttering hearts, the lovers approach the beloved, called by his whistling like pigeons that throng with flapping wings around the balcony. And the pigeon that has dwelt on the Friend's roof is more precious than anything in the world.

Birds and flowers seem to compete in beauty during these early spring days in Konya. Fascinated by the dazzling beauty of the peacock, Rumi compares spring to a peacock in pride who struts about out of love for the Friend's face, for both garden and peacock participate in his loveliness. The colorful bird opens his marvelous feathers "like lovers' hearts"; dancing, he induces man's soul to dance and thus merges with the great complex of images related to spring.

Maulana knows, of course, that the peacock may well be accused of vaingloriousness, and thus the *Mathnawī* relates the story of the peacock who wanted to repent and began to pluck out his colorful plumage. A loving Sufi warned him not to do so, for his beauty was, after all, also created by God, and his feathers are placed as bookmarks in copies of the Koran.

All year long, mice (symbols of the lower instincts) run through the granaries and kitchens, but in spring even a mouse can fall in love, though, as Maulana tells us in the *Mathnawī,* she may choose a wrong object of love, namely a frog—with the result that both perish miserably, just as the spirit perishes when it is bound to the lower soul, the *nafs*. Hedgehogs also inhabit the gardens. They look small but can increase their size in times of danger by erecting their bristles: are they not a good likeness of the faithful believer who becomes stronger in adversity?

It seems the only creatures who do not enjoy spring are the bats: they hate the sun, or rather deny its very existence, just as the unloving inhabitants of Konya hated Shamsuddin and claimed that "the sun has died." But is not the bats' hatred a sign of a man's true greatness, as the Prophet once said?

In spring, after the snow has vanished, it is less difficult for a caravan to reach the Seljukid capital. The travelers who stop at the caravansaries by the roadside may see water gushing forth from the mouths of stone animals near the gate; but only those who do not know the working of God without secondary causes will believe that a stone animal can produce water out of itself. Those of insight will see here, as everywhere, the hidden hand of the Creator.

The camel drivers' song was heard far across the plains, and the camels began to run toward their goal. Carrying precious salt from the nearby Salt Lake or loads of sugarcane from Egypt, homeland of sugar, or perhaps bales of silk from Shushtar in southern Iran, the camels were intoxicated by the song of their drivers and despite their heavy burdens would seem almost to dance. Maulana often sings of these patient animals as symbols of the soul who moves to the dwelling place of the Beloved. When it hears the driver's voice—that is, the Prophet's or the spiritual leader's call—it moves joyously over desert and steppe:

> See the nose-ring of the lovers in your hand—
> I am in this row of camels, day and night! (D 302)

Yet in the hand of Love one can even see a long line of lions walk, with the Beloved's string in their noses, obedient like camels (D 2177).

On a warm spring day such as this, the nobility might take up their outdoor activities. Polo was played in the capital as it was everywhere between the Hindu Kush and Egypt, and in *Fīhi mā fīhi* Maulana compares the exercises in this game to the representation in worldly form of spiritual values. The poor lover (or his head) is like the polo ball that is driven mercilessly across the field by the mallet, whose shape, again, reminded poets of the beloved's curled tresses, which sent their heads spinning. But Rumi does not use this image as frequently as do other poets of his time.

Other high-ranking people might begin at this time to hunt

with falcons. The disciple's training on the mystical path at the hand of the master is compared, in *Fīhi mā fīhi,* to the training of a useless fledgling that must endure much hardship until he is worthy of serving his lord properly. Then, however, it may happen that the beautiful bird is trapped by an old woman, the Mistress World of medieval imagery, and almost forgets his home, or else he may fall among owls and ravens (as Suhrawardi the Master of Illumination told before Rumi): there, held prisoner in the hibernal world, he gradually remembers the master's palace and finally hears once more the sound of the drum calling him back: "How should that falcon not fly back when the sound of the drum conveys to him the call *irji'ī,* 'Return!'?"

After much suffering and hard education, the falcon at last becomes a symbol of the *nafs muṭma'inna,* the "soul at peace" (Sura 89/27), who is called home by its Creator, and in a touching scene, Maulana shows us the proud bird, sitting on his master's fist and rubbing his head against the Lord's breast, asking forgiveness for his trespasses. (M II 334) Elsewhere, the falcon can also be the bird of ecstasy, the overwhelming power of divine Love that carries off the timid human heart just as a falcon seizes its prey.

When he spoke of these birds and observed the great variety of songbirds and others, Maulana may at times have thought of another favorite soul-bird—one, however, that was not at home in Anatolia, although it was probably kept in the homes of the wealthy. Like the peacock originally connected with India, the parrot also assumed a special role in the mystical universe of Muslim poets. His green plumage shows that the parrot certainly belongs to paradise; he is a wise bird who continues to warn and instruct, just as he did in the fables of his Indian homeland; his words are sweet, and he is "sugar chewing" like the lover who thinks of his beloved. How should the dung-eating crow know that the parrot lives on sugar? The first represents the matter-bound soul; the second, the soul that knows the joys of spiritual sweetness. The parrot's role as soul-bird becomes evident in Rumi's famous story in the first book of the *Mathnawī* wherein a parrot, from his cage in a merchant's house, asks his owner to convey greetings to his bird relatives in India when the owner visits there. The merchant carries out his promise, and the parrot who hears of his imprisoned relative drops dead from horror. Returning, the man has to relay this sad news to his own bird, who immediately keels over in turn. The despairing merchant opens the cage to dispose of his pet's body, but as soon as the parrot regains his freedom, he comes alive and informs the owner that his relative's message was this: "Die before ye die!" By following this Sufi advice and dying to one's own base qualities before dying in the body, one is released from the prison of matter.

The parrot also represents the spiritual disciple: just as the parrot is taught to speak by means of a mirror, so the disciple is instructed in the language of the spirit by his master, who, like a mirror, reflects all spiritual qualities.

Perhaps Maulana saw all this with his inner eye as he strolled through the springtime gardens of Konya and observed the chirping birds, the lively rabbits and cunning foxes, and listened with disgust to the donkeys whose braying the Koran calls "the ugliest voice" (Sura 31/18). Typical creature of the world of matter, sensual and delighting in filth—how could a donkey enjoy spiritual beauty or feel the refreshing breeze that comes like the breath of Jesus? No, Maulana did not care if a donkey got lost; in fact, one should be happy to be rid of such an animal! And he observed other creatures: insects that throng in a bowl of sour milk on a warm day (would not the souls throng like that in the Divine Presence?). Like flies in honey, they would be unable to remember their outward limbs, submerged as they are in the sweetness of union. There were also other, dangerous little creatures, worms that despite their tiny size could hollow out whole trees; then only the tree's bark remained—just as Love takes possession of the human body and soul so that only one's name is left, nothing else. . . .

Early in the morning he heard the rooster calling the believers to their morning prayer. Is this useful creature not in reality an *angelos*—Maulana actually used the Greek word!—rather than an ordinary bird? And as the days passed, packs of hungry stray dogs clustered together in search of food, resembling humans who think only of their daily bread. Looking at them, he thought of the old Sufi saying that "the world is carrion and those who seek it are like dogs." But even these miserable creatures can teach us humans something, for they are faithful and loyal and can be purified in the company of the saintly, like the faithful dog of the Seven Sleepers (Sura 18/21). And when they are starving they ask for bread by wagging their tails—how then should man, who is so much higher than the animals, not "wag his tail to ask something from God"?

Spring is also the time when children run out again to play in the streets after being confined so long in their narrow houses. They especially love to spin nuts, yet they care nothing for the kernel, which contains the very soul of the nut, the precious oil: are they not like the scholars who interest themselves in external sciences only, or like those who recite the Koran in technically flawless style without understanding its deeper meaning? The little boys fill their skirts with dirt and stones to play with, and may become so engrossed in their games that they leave their jackets behind or forget how to find the way back home, where their loving mother, representative of Divine Loving-kindness, awaits their return.

Rumi enjoyed listening to the silent talk of nature, yet he knew that all this was but a colorful veil before the Beloved's face, the only thing that remains forever while "everything upon earth is transient" (Sura 28/88).

> In the garden are hundreds of charming beloveds
> And roses and tulips dancing around
> And limpid water running in the brook.
> All this is a pretext—it is He alone!

If that sounds pantheistic, we may wonder how Maulana's son and biographer, Sultan Walad, explains this view:

> Whoever possesses that light which the angels had is not taken aback by Adam's clay, but sees the light of God in Adam. Indeed, whoever is more perfected will see God in stones and straw and wood, in everything and in the atoms, as Bayezid Bistami saw it and said: "I never saw anything without seeing God in it." (VN 171)

There is another story that complements Maulana's ecstatic spring songs: it is the story of a Sufi (originally the great woman saint Rabi'a of Basra) who sat at home on a glorious spring day and refused to step outside in order to admire God's work in nature, for

> The gardens and the fruits are in the heart—
> Only the reflection of His kindness is in this water
> and clay. (M IV 1357f.)

And yet this latter verse does not fully convey Maulana's personal attitude. For:

> Thanks to the gaze of the sun, the soil became a tulip
> bed—
> To sit at home is now a plague, a plague! (D 1349)

As much as he knew that the passage of seasons is an external event ("Winter and July are states of the body," D 1528) that does not touch those souls who belong entirely to the world of spirit; as much as he realized that gardens and roses are a mere reflection of the eternal beauty of the Divine Beloved, and that he who looks at the garden sees the beauty of the gardener—still he was endowed with the gift to see traces of this beauty everywhere, for God has put His signs "in the horizons and in yourselves" (Sura 41/53). Rumi knew well that the subtlety of spirit needs matter to become visible, and through his eyes his friends learned to see the glory of the Divine Beloved everywhere, especially in spring, when the divine breeze, the rain of Grace, and the Sun of reality work together to melt the snow of coarse matter and call every atom to the intoxicated dance of spiritual resurrection.

5

The Hidden Treasure

Maulana's Thoughts about God and His Creation

THE BASIS, CENTER, AND GOAL OF MAULANA'S thought is God, the One and Infinite, whose essence can never be reached, rather should never be the theme of thought and discussion:

> Whatever you can think is perishable.
> That which enters no thought, that's God! (M II 3107)

And yet this God manifests Himself everywhere, for He is active and omniscient. Maulana recognizes Him as the God of the Koran, and in particular as the God as described in the Throne Verse (Sura 2/256), which calls him *al-ḥayy al-qayyūm,* "The Living, through Himself Subsisting." He is not a *prima causa,* the immovable being behind everything yet far removed from the world He has created through His word; rather He is the source of all love, or perhaps even dynamic Love Himself—and ultimately even transcends the manifestations of Love.

Maulana's poetry and prose are an attempt to circumambulate Him whose work is so evident in the universe and who has promised mankind that He will hear its prayers (Sura 40/62), the One who has sent His prophets to instruct humanity after He once had created the world out of nothing and never ceases to create new things. It is impossible to prove God's existence by logical and intellectual means, as a story in *Fīhi mā fīhi* makes clear: Maulana tells that one morning a learned, philosophically minded scholar came to Shams-i Tabriz and told him, "I have proved God's existence with a categorial proof!" The next morning Shams told his friends, "Tonight I saw the angels descending in my dream. They blessed this man and said, 'He has proved God's existence—at least he has not done harm to any creature!' "

In a *hadīth qudsī,* an extra-Koranic word, God calls Himself a hidden treasure: "I was a hidden treasure and I wanted to be known, so I created the world!" (*kuntu kanzan makhfiyyan* . . .). Sometimes the phrase "I wanted to be known" is replaced, in Sufi circles, by "I wanted to be loved." God is a treasure of mercy, inexhaustible, just as He is a treasure of beauty. This beauty reflects itself in the world, which can be seen as a mirror for Him, provided one looks at the side that is turned toward God; for its rear side is worthless, although the decorations on the metal may seem attractive to those who look only at the surface.

But, the philosophers ask, "Before heaven and earth existed, before Throne and Footstool were created—where was God?" Maulana rebukes those who ask such questions, which he considers utterly absurd: He was always there, without any Where or When. In *Fīhi mā fīhi,* a number of his remarks concerning philosophers (a species he disliked thoroughly) are preserved. Among the problems they brought to the fore was the traditional discussion of whether or not the world was eternal. Maulana answers them with the parable of the architect: the architect is subtler than the house he plans to build, and we cannot imagine what is in his mind unless we see the actual construction of the well-planned house itself, which proves the wise architect's activity, or rather his existence. Only nearsighted worldly creatures could believe that the world is eternal: are they not like insects or mice who inhabit a house and, owing to their short lifespan, imagine that the house has been there from eternity? By contrast, the human inhabitants who have lived in the house some fifty or sixty years have seen how the master conceived its plan, how it was built and furnished; they know that the house was created in time. In the same way, the saints, whose spirits dwelt with God before creation and who once enjoyed undivided unity in God, know that the world came into existence at a point when God deemed it necessary. In this respect Maulana follows his admired model Sana'i, who once wrote:

> From prime matter, *hayūlā,* and First Cause
> You do not find the way into the Lord's presence!

The world in which we live—so Maulana thinks—is like floating jetsam, like a constantly moving sea that is "decked out fair," as the Koran tells us (Sura 3/14): we may enjoy it for a time, but we should never forget the Creator. Sometimes Rumi takes up certain older ascetic images whereby the early Sufis voiced their hatred of the world—this dunghill, which is enjoyed only by pigs (that is, the immature), while the true seekers hunt the gazelle "Soul," the lovely musk deer whose fragrance guides them to the eternal home.

But Maulana is not always so negative; in fact, he sees something positive everywhere, and the world—as long as it is seen as the mirror of God, or as long as one is aware of its transient character—is necessary in order for God to show His power, and for man to develop into something higher and more spiritual. At the center of Maulana's theology—or theodicy—stands his unshakable faith in God's wisdom and mercy; but he knows very well that the Eternal One can only display His activities dialectically. The very word of creation, *Kun* ("Be!"), points to this secret: it is written in Arabic with two letters, *kāf* and *nūn,* and can be easily compared to a two-colored yarn that appears in the fabric of the manifest universe and hides the essential Divine Unity. God manifests Himself, as the Muslims long knew, under two aspects, His beauty (*jamāl*) and His power, or majesty (*jalāl*). These two aspects correspond closely to what the twentieth-century theologian Rudolf Otto calls the *fascinans,* the fascinating, and the *tremendum,* the tremendous, awe-inspiring aspect of the Numinous. The Most Beautiful Names of God, as they are found in the Koran, point to this constant interplay of Mercy and Wrath, Beauty and Power: God is *al-qābiḍ* and *al-bāsiṭ,* the One who presses together and the One who expands; He is *al-muḥyī* and *al-mumīt,* He who gives Life and He who makes die, the One who raises and who lowers, who is both loving and overpowering. This duality is inherent in creation, for the moment that creation came into existence, the absolute Unity was split into a subject and an object, into Creator and creature, and in order to keep life going, the cosmos needs this constant shift from the positive to the negative pole, the alternating movements of inhaling and exhaling, of the heartbeat, and of day and night, life and death (or, in the terms of Chinese philosophy, *yang* and *yin*). One pole cannot exist without the other. Maulana teaches his audience this simple rule, invites them to see life and the unfolding of ever-new possibilities that emerge from this interplay of contrasts, for, as the Koran says, "He is every day in some work" (Sura 55/29); God's activity never ceases, and "Neither slumber nor sleep overcomes Him" (Sura 2/256). He is aware of the needs of His creatures and shows Himself in ever-new epiphanies, whether in the radiance of a cheerful spring day or in the misery of decay and suffering. It is He who continually offers signs so that we may understand His work, for He knows at every moment exactly what each one needs.

The totality of this view may seem difficult for a skeptical mind to accept. Why, then, would there be so much suffering on earth? What is the meaning of illness, hunger, catastrophes? Maulana's answer is simple—perhaps too simplistic for a modern inquisitive mind, and yet clearly born from his deep conviction that there is a meaning in everything. God, who has called Himself *khayr al-mākirīn,* "the best of the plotters" (Sura 3/54, 8/30), has ways that no human mind can understand, and His grace is often "hidden in wrath, as a precious carnelian is hidden in the dust." He may destroy for the sake of rebuilding, and when He abrogates a verse of the Koran, he does so in order to bring something better in its place. The sometimes destructive acts of the saints through whom He works give proof of this deeper wisdom, as may be seen from the story of Khidr, the mysterious guide of travelers, whose behavior appeared criminal to Moses but was rooted in profound meaning (Sura 18/64–81). This attitude shapes Maulana's answer to the problem of suffering: a physician does not approve of illness and suffering, yet he wants people to be ill in order to show his skill in curing them; the baker dislikes people being hungry, yet he wants people to have need of bread so that he may prove his skill in providing them with bread. This simple answer may not satisfy us, yet the argumentation comes close to the Christian idea that God does not approve of sin and yet needs the sinner to show His mercy and forgiveness—an idea that is also expressed, in a somewhat concealed form, by Maulana's vision of the water's longing for the dirty so that it can purify them properly.

Another question that has worried people throughout the ages: Why do some people suffer, undergo punishment or affliction, and appear bound for Hell, while others seem perfectly happy and blessed and in hope of attaining Paradise? All, Maulana holds, are witnesses to God's majesty and glory. For He is the mighty king, and a king has in His realm robes of honor as well as gallows. When the king bestows a fine robe upon one who has done well, the recipient bears witness to His kindness; equally, when He hangs a criminal, the man on the gallows is, as Rumi says, "a preacher to people" of the ruler's justice. Thus His hand is behind whatever may happen in the universe.

God's majesty and beauty, His wrath and His kindness, are manifested in every moment; indeed, they form the warp and woof of life, for there is "nothing that does not proclaim His glory" (Sura 17/44). God is never unjust, for justice is one of His innate qualities, and even events that appear unjust or incomprehensible to an amazed humanity have their deeper meaning, known only to

Him. Everything praises Him in its own mute eloquence, whether it be stone or animal, plant or human, and even those who suffer in Hell remember Him more intensely than they ever did during their lifetimes, when they forgot or resisted Him. Maulana's argumentation here has a daring ring:

> The inhabitants of Hell will be happier in Hell than they were in the world, for in the world they had no idea of God, whereas in Hell they will think of Him—and nothing can be sweeter than knowledge of God. (*Fīhi mā fīhi,* chap. 63)

To know him, to be aware of Him, is the greatest blessing—and for those who have eyes to see, everything is a sign pointing to Him, for "We have placed signs into the horizons and in yourselves" (Sura 41/53). They know that all atoms are His armies whom He can send wherever He will. Maulana trusts that the wise Creator knows exactly what His creatures need. Certain small animals that live underground have no eyes or ears, for they do not need them. Likewise, God leaves certain people without the inner senses with which to reach Him, for He knows that they are much happier in the darkness of this world and would only be embarrassed if they could see what is beyond it.

Just like the sun, the Creator, Nourisher, and Judge, the One and Unique, is far too glorious to be seen without veils, and for this reason the word *rūpūsh* "cover for the face," appears frequently in Maulana's poetry. Everything is in some sense a veil behind which God is hidden. The same applies to His activities: although He creates everything without a mediator, He has placed over each of His creations what appear to be secondary causes. The traveler on the road who perceives a cloud of dust from afar does not recognize the horseman who is hidden by the dusty veil. Similarly, one who stands on the ocean's shore may see the never-resting foam and the rising and falling billows without ever understanding the actual depth of the sea. In one of his greatest visionary poems

Maulana describes a scene in which he gazes at the unfathomable ocean, from which flecks of foam appear like figures and forms, only to disappear again when the depths call them back:

> The ocean billowed, and lo!
> > Eternal Wisdom appeared
> And cast forth its voice and cried out . . .
> > That was how it was and became.
> The ocean was all filled with foam
> > and every fleck of this foam
> Produced a figure like this,
> > and was a body like that,
> And every body-shaped fleck
> > that heard a sign from that sea,
> It melted and then returned
> > into the ocean of souls . . .
>
> (D 649)

This vision leads us to an important aspect of Maulana's thought. The poet continually emphasizes, in good Koranic terms, the *creatio ex nihilo,* the concept that God created everything out of nothing. And yet one aspect of this concept at times poses difficulties to our understanding. It is the term *'adam,* "not-being," "nonexistence." Like his father, Baha'-i Walad, in whose thought *'adam* held an important place, Maulana too uses the term repeatedly when he speaks of the relation between God, humanity, and creation. References abound to the "ocean of *'adam*" out of which army after army of created things appears in this world, and one often gets the impression that *'adam* is something out of which everything is formed: nonexistence that is, paradoxically, the stuff out of which the existing world is created. For, as Maulana says in a lyrical poem: "To be nothing is the precondition of being" (D 2642). Nothingness itself thus serves the Creator as the repository of everything that will be created, and everything in 'adam yearns for being, enters Being, as it were, in an ecstatic dance (D 1832). God is by far greater than 'adam, and so is Love. For this reason, 'adam is hardly to be seen as the Divine Essence, the *deus absconditus* or "desert of the Godhead," as Meister Eckhart would call it half a century later in Germany; it is rather "the treasure trove of God's work from which He brings forth gifts at every moment" (M V 1023f.), the treasure trove "out of which comes the gold, in cash money" (D 709). 'Adam is the house that provides God, its Creator, with infinite possibilities for the future.

> Waves of being come out of it constantly,
> so that from their movement a hundred mills are set in
> motion. (D 155)

For Maulana,

> Being and not-being are brothers, as contrasts are hidden in
> each other:
> Did not the Koran say: "He brings forth the living from the
> dead" (Sura 31/18)? (M V 1018–19)

However, there is yet another use of the term 'adam in Maulana's work, one that may bring us closer to the concept of the Absolute Essence of God: not only do things and beings emerge from 'adam, they also long to return to it, just as the drop yearns to return to the ocean from which it once rose. And "though every animal is afraid of 'adam, the heart longs for it" (D 2480).

> Return before Him and become 'adam,
> for 'adam is the mine of the soul

—but not of a soul "which is only worry and grief!" (D 331). Even more clearly the attraction of 'adam is expressed in these lines:

> For 'adam is an ocean, we are like fishes,
> and Being is the net . . . (D 734)

In this respect *'adam* is the undifferentiated Unity, the "reed bed" for which the reed flute longs, and the final goal of everything in Creation. Here one may think of 'Attar, who at the end of his *Ushturnāma* shows how the puppeteer breaks all the puppets once the play is over and stores the broken pieces again in the dark box of Unity. But for Maulana, there is something beyond *'adam* and existence:

> Love has the ears of *'adam* in its hand, and both—
> nonexistence and existence—are dependent upon it, *tufayl*
>
> > (D 1019)

Even more:

> Even though a thousand worlds would issue from *'adam,*
> to the page of Love [God] they would be like beauty spots,
> not more. (D 2234)

And Maulana has expressed his feeling of absolute dependence upon the Beloved, in a line that is typical of his nonrational approach:

> You know yourself that I, without You, am not-being, not-
> being (*'adam*).
> Not-being is capable of being—I am less than that! (D 1432)

Concepts such as these are typical of the so-called "mystical" approach to God and to religious experience in general, and to a certain extent verses of this kind surely reflect Maulana's Neoplatonic heritage. This mystical approach is connected with water imagery, whereby the ocean is considered the ideal symbol for the unfathomable depth of not-being in its positive aspect. But as important as Maulana's numerous verses about *'adam* may be, they do not represent his final word, nor do they signal his only way to approach the mystery of the Divine. For Rumi experienced God also as the active and willing power, as the "personal" God who is

Love, Love in its highest manifestations—Love that can be as kind
as it can be cruel, and that uses various methods to educate the
lover. Maulana teaches his readers to contemplate this aspect of
the ever-active God, who shapes the world according to a plan
that He alone knows.

Like all Muslims, and in particular all Sufis, Maulana was well
aware of the importance of the Divine Names, which he mentions
as perfect expressions of God's complementary activities. However,
he never indulges in the mysticism of names that was so common
in Sufi fraternities, and it seems—for we have no actual documen-
tation of his use or nonuse of the Names in the practice of *dhikr,*
the "recollection" of religious names and formulas—that he did
not much dwell upon the qualities of the Divine Names or their
effects upon one who repeats them thousands of times. As much
as he lost himself in the name of Shams, which served almost as a
magic formula to conjure up the lost beloved, he apparently did
not use the traditional sacred names of God in the same way. For
him, the Divine Names represent models of ethical qualities: when
hearing the name *al-baṣīr,* "the Seeing," one should remember that
God sees everything, just as He hears everything and hence calls
Himself *as-samī',* "the Hearing." The names that reflect His
forgiveness and kindness, such as *al-ghaffār,* "the All-forgiving," or
al-wadūd," "the Loving," remind us to follow the model set forth
by these names, as the tradition tells us: *takhallaqū bi-akhlāq Allāh,*
"Qualify yourselves with the qualities of God." The names are
given to teach and guide us; here again, Maulana is close to the
interpretation of the Names given by al-Ghazzali, whose work he
knew well.

Of course, some of the Names readily offer themselves to
poetical elaboration: when God is called *al-muṣawwir,* "the Shaper"
or "Painter," it is easy to see Him as the great artist who shows
His mastery in rendering the beautiful and the ugly with equal
skill. In a related image very dear to Islam, in which tradition
calligraphy is the most respected art form, Maulana sees God as

the master calligrapher in whose hand the heart is like a pen, and the ḥadīth that "the heart of the believer is between two fingers of the Merciful" offered him additional support for this comparison.

> My heart became like a pen
>   that's in the Beloved's fingers:
> Tonight he may write a *Z,*
>   perhaps tomorrow, a *B.*
> He cuts and prepares his pen well
>   to write in *riqa'* and *naskh*;
> The pen says: "Lo, I obey,
>   for you know best what to do."
> Sometimes he blackens its face,
>   he wipes it then in his hair,
> He holds it now upside down,
>   sometimes he writes with it too . . . (D 2530)

For the reed pen has to be cut according to the rules, and every style of calligraphy, be it the normal cursive hand of *naskh* or the involved *riqā'* used in the chancery, requires a special slanting and cutting of the pen's nib. Thus God trims everyone according to the needs of the page He is going to write, and in the end all the different letters, between *A* and *Z,* will form a meaningful text whose content they themselves cannot know. The pen can do only one thing: put its head obediently on the paper when the artist guides it in unknown directions.

God is also the great weaver on whose loom colorful and marvelous fabrics are woven, and Maulana, who lived in an area well known for its fine tapestries and rugs, employs the symbol of the weaver most skillfully in his consolation of those who try to act according to their own wishes and must confront the final breakdown of their schemes.

> Weave not, like spiders, nets from grief's saliva
> In which the woof and warp are both decaying.
> But give the grief to Him who granted it,
> And do not talk about it anymore.
> When you are silent, His speech is your speech;
> When you don't weave, the weaver will be He. (D 922)

Even in his moments of deepest grief, Maulana never loses hope in God's eternal grace and wisdom. He learned in the many weeks, months, and years of suffering in Love that a secret pattern lay behind all of the world's trials, and in his own life he realized the truth:

> And if He closes before you
>   all passes and all ways,
> He'll show a hidden pathway
>   which no one yet has known.

It is perhaps this aspect of his teaching that has endeared him to millions of readers, and it is here that his work contrasts strongly with that of his predecessor in mystical poetry, Fariduddin 'Attar. 'Attar's beautiful Persian tales often contain an element of social criticism, even of outcries against God, who made the world so crooked and should have known better; and although 'Attar usually discovers some sweet consolation, yet the haze of melancholia is always visible in his verse. Rumi, on the other hand, emerges at the end of his stories always with a triumphant Yes to God's power, kindness, and wisdom. An example of the contrasting approaches of the two poets can be seen in their varying presentation of the story of the dervish in Herat who looked on as the retinue of a prince passed by in majestic array and with everyone rigged to the nines, bearing glittering arms, and cried out that the Lord should learn from these people how to look after His friends. Rumi, in his telling, adds that the Divine Voice thereupon reminded the dervish that a human being might provide him with a hat and a coat, but that God provides something far more precious—that is, a head and a body. The same argumentation occurs in one of the final stories of the *Mathnawī* (M VI 3124ff.), when the complaining individual finally realizes:

> Although the master was quite generous,
> Yet it could not compare, Lord, with Your gift.
> He gave the hat, and You the head with reason,
> He gave a cloak, You gave the limbs, the body.
> He gave a mule, and You the rider Reason.
> The master gave a candle, You the eyesight,
> He gave me dainties; You, the appetite. . . .

The feeling that everything is in the hands of God, who knows best how to use His creatures, appears in ecstatic poems in the *Dīwān* as it appears in the very last part of the *Mathnawī*—as though Maulana, in the final phase of his life, wanted to sum up his feelings and experiences beyond all the different tales he had been telling his audience. Thus, filled with love, he sings:

> If He makes me a goblet, I become a goblet,
> If He makes me a dagger, I become a dagger.
> If He makes me a fountain, then I shall give water,
> If He makes me fire, then I shall give heat.
> If He makes me rain, I'll bring forth the harvest,
> If He makes me a needle, I pierce the body.
> If He makes me a snake, I'll produce poison,
> If He makes me His friend, I shall serve only Him. (M V 1686)

God can do whatever He wants, and His creation reflects in a sense the infinite possibilities of His essence. How can one describe Him properly? Here Maulana borrows from Sana'i the story of the blind men who, led before an elephant, attempt to find out what this wondrous beast might look like. According to whatever part their hands had touched they describe the animal to their companions as a throne or a hubblebubble, a fan or a spout—and not one can imagine how the whole animal might be shaped. This parable, taken over by Sana'i from Indian sources, has remained a favorite with all who know that any attempt to describe the Divine is futile. In a more lyrical expression, Maulana tells the same truth in almost playful words:

> Oh seize the hem of His favor,
>   for suddenly He will flee!
> But do not draw Him like arrows,
>   for from the bow He will flee.
> Look—all the shapes He assumes, and
>   what kinds of tricks He plays!
> In form He may well be present,
>   but from the soul He will flee.
> You seek Him high in His heaven—
>   He shines like the moon in a lake,
> But if you enter the water,
>   up to the sky He will flee.
> You seek Him in Where-no-place is—
>   then He gives signs of His place:
> But if you seek Him in places,
>   to Where-no-place He will flee.
> As arrows fly from the bowstring
>   and like the bird of your thought . . .
> You know for sure: from the doubting
>   the Absolute One will flee.
> "I'll flee from this one and that one,
>   but not out of weariness:
> I fear that My beauty, so lovely,
>   from this and from that may well flee.
> For like the wind I am flighty,
>   and I love the rose, like the breeze,
> But out of fear of the autumn,

> you see, the rose too will flee!"
> His name will flee when it sees you
>   intent on pronouncing it
> So that you cannot tell others:
>   "Look here, such a person will flee!"
> He'll flee from you if you try then
>   to sketch His image and form—
> The drawing will flee from the tablet,
>   the sign from the heart will flee!

Maulana certainly knew the futility of attempting to capture the vision of the Divine. But he knew also, as Sultan Walad says in the first pages of the *Waladnāma,* that God is hidden because His radiance is all too great: like the sun, yet more eminent than the sun, He cannot be seen because He is too manifest—a paradox that was used among the Sufis throughout the ages. For this reason, the poet must turn to the use of metaphor to speak of God, of His *kibriyā,* His stunning glory, the radiant "cloak" of His essence. *Kibriyā*—a word whose very sound suggests something strong and positive—seems to be the counterpart of *'adam,* the dark "box of Unity," but both aspects of the Divine belong together. Therefore it is not surprising that Maulana's metaphors and symbols at times are contradictory. How can one express the One who cannot be imagined except in paradoxes?

Yet despite the feeling that God eludes the limitation of every human description, Maulana's faith in Him is unshakable, for he knows that whatever may happen is initiated by God; it is always He who takes the first step. It is He who addressed not-yet-created humanity with the words "Am I not your Lord?" (Sura 7/172), and it was He who "taught Adam the names" (Sura 2/32).

> Lovers do not themselves seek and yearn—
> In all the world there is no one seeking but He! (D 425)

Maulana sums up this center of his theology (if one may call it that) in a line that has been taken over into the mystical literatures of Islam:

> Not only the thirsty seek the water—
> The water also seeks the thirsty. (M I 1704)

He who is the Beloved is also the Lover, and His grace will grasp man in an unexpected moment, never to let him go again. In this regard Maulana tells a sad little story in the *Dīwān* that he repeats in *Fīhi mā fīhi* (or the sequence may have been the other way round):

> A schoolteacher who was so utterly destitute that he had only a cotton shirt to wear even on cold winter days was standing by a rushing mountain stream when he suddenly saw a bear in the water. The animal had fallen into the gushing waves high up in the mountains and was now being carried by the torrential waters down to the village. The schoolchildren, pitying their teacher, told him to jump into the water and seize the fine fur coat that had apparently arrived there as a much-appreciated gift. Out of despair he jumped into the water, but the bear, still very much alive, grasped him and drew him close to its body. When the horrified children saw this, they asked the teacher to let the fur coat go, but he answered: "I'll let the fur coat go, but the fur coat does not let me go!"

Maulana continues, in *Fīhi mā fīhi*: once Divine Grace has grasped you, it will never let you go!

Divine Grace is seeking mankind, but also strong faith is required to accept it. Living faith enables the believer to make the last step in the direction of a fierce lion and to caress him: the lion devours those who shiver and dare not approach him, but those who are brave and whose faith is unshaking will be able to become his close friends. It is this strong faith, born of Love, that Maulana preaches through his poetry and prose: once one has such faith, one will understand God's wisdom and the perfection of all things, and everything will fall into place. However, there is no way of understanding the working of God intellectually; the philosophers' claims are so much straw and wooden chips on the water, and the theologians with their analytical minds do not perceive the deeper reasons for life either. Maulana has attempted to show at least one way to the unfathomable mystery of the Living and Self-subsisting God, and has tried to invent ever-new images to lead his listeners to it; yet it seems to me that the most moving approach to the relationship between the seeking human and his Creator and Lord is found in a chapter in *Fīhi mā fīhi,* where Maulana takes up the old story of moth and candle, first used in Sufism by the martyr-mystic al-Hallaj, some three hundred and fifty years before Maulana. Speaking of the impossible task of recognizing God, Rumi says:

> Reason is that which is ever restless and without peace day and night from thinking and worrying and trying to comprehend God, even though God is incomprehensible and beyond our understanding. Reason is like a moth, and the Beloved like a candle. Though the moth cast itself into the flame and burn and be destroyed, yet the true moth is such that it cannot exist without the candle, much as it may suffer from the pain of its immolation. If there were any creature like the moth that could do without the light of the candle and that would refrain from casting itself into this light, it would not be a true moth; and if the moth should cast itself into the candle's light and the candle not burn it, that would not be a true candle.

Therefore the human being who can live without God and who does not undertake any effort is not a real human being; and if he could comprehend God, then that would not be God. That one is the true human being who never rests from striving and who wanders forever without rest around the light of God's beauty and majesty. And God is the one who consumes man and annihilates him, and no reason can comprehend Him.

6

A Donkey's Tail with Angel's Wings

> Man's situation is like this: an angel's wing was brought and tied
> to a donkey's tail so that the donkey perchance might also become
> an angel, thanks to the radiance of the angel's company.
>
> *(Fīhi mā fīhi, chap. 26)*

THIS IS AN IMPRESSIVE IMAGE, for it portrays the human condition,
the fact that the only creature with a certain amount of free will
is situated between beast and angel, between the world of pure
matter and that of pure spirit. If he follows his lower instincts, he
will fall deeper than any animal, for the animals are constrained in
their actions and have no choice. If, however, he purifies himself
and develops his God-given spiritual qualities, he will reach a
station higher than the angels, for angels, too, cannot act according
to their own inclination; their role of constant worship and
obedience is once and for all prescribed. Humans, however, have
to wander along an extremely narrow path as they choose between
good and evil, matter and spirit; they are, as Maulana says, like
ducks, which belong to both water and earth; or else they are half
honeybee, half snake, capable of producing both honey and venom.
Did not the angels cry out in horror when the Lord told them at
the beginning of time that He would place a vice-regent on earth,

whereupon they foresaw that the new creature would be "bloodshedding and ignorant" (Sura 2/31)? But God knew better what He was planning, and so the angels had to prostrate themselves before the newly created Adam, who thus became *masjūd al-malā'ika*, "the one before whom the angels fell down." He was singled out by the Divine Word in the Koran: *karamnā*, "We have honored the children of Adam" (Sura 17/70). Maulana reminds his listeners time and again of this Divine Word, and he sees the greatest danger to humanity in the risk of their forgetting the high position allotted to them by God. God "taught Adam the names" (Sura 2/32). Neither angel nor beast but only human beings are aware of the names of the created things, so that they can address them and rule over them (for to know someone's name means to have power over him). What is even more important— so the Sufis say—human beings were also taught the mystery of the Divine Names that they may call upon God, who can be approached through His ninety-nine Most Beautiful Names.

But alas, we all too easily forget the high rank to which we were assigned! Maulana exemplifies this with a story (M V 2547ff.) taken from the panegyrist Anwari and which he elaborates: A man was seen running fearfully through the streets; another asked him the reason for his strange behavior. "But," replied the first, "have you not heard that the king is hunting asses today?" "But you are no ass," said the neighbor. Whereupon the first man answered that one could never know—and perhaps the king would not know either! In reply, the neighbor reminded him that he was not a donkey but a Jesus, a fully spiritual being that has only its material body, the "husk," in common with an animal. The contrasting images *Jesus/donkey, spirit/matter*—favorites of Maulana's—are cleverly presented in this story. For Maulana never tires of repeating (especially in *Fīhi mā fīhi*) that the greatest danger and in a sense also the greatest sin for the human being lies in the tendency to neglect his spiritual part, to forget that he is "honored by God." Is he not like a stupid person who owns a beautiful, gem-studded Indian sword or precious dagger, but rather than using it nobly as it was meant to be used, cuts rotten meat with it or hammers it into the wall like a nail to hang an old broken gourd on it? Or he resembles someone who uses a golden pot to boil turnips, when he could have bought hundreds of common pots for a tiny part of that gold. But alas, that is what most people do: they are so busy with their worldly occupations that they forget to cultivate their real self, that part that was given as a special gift from God, who "breathed into him from His own breath" (Sura 15/29), as the Koran states several times. It is the Divine *amāna,* the "entrusted good" that is the most important and at the same time the most endangered element in human beings, as Sura 33/72 says: "Verily We offered the *amāna* to mountains and heaven and earth and they did not accept it, but man accepted it, and verily he is ignorant, cruel." For man did not know what he was receiving, or how heavy the burden would be (and indeed, Muslim theologians and mystics have pondered through the ages what exactly this "entrusted good" might have been). For Rumi the *amāna* is the gift of responsibility, of free choice, of a human being's ability to recognize the spiritual aspects of his being and develop them. Those who forget or neglect the *amāna* are in a dangerous position; they may run about in hundreds of different pursuits, but so long as they do not care for the precious divine gift they carry within themselves, hidden like a golden goblet in a bag filled with straw, or a jewel in a dungheap—so long as they neglect it or are not even aware of it, nothing is of avail.

Maulana explains this in a story in *Fīhi mā fīhi*: A king had a somewhat imbecile son whom he entrusted to the masters of all crafts, including astrology and magic. After the son had completed his schooling, the king sent for him and, hiding a golden ring in his fist, asked, "What do I keep in my hand?" The boy answered correctly, "It is round, hollow, and yellow." "Bravo!" exclaimed the king. "Now that you know all the particulars, tell me what it is!" And the prince answered, "It must be a millstone!" Most humans resemble this foolish prince, says Maulana. One knows all the external signs of things but is unaware of the essence of life: thinking of our particularities, we do not remember our immortal individual soul, the *khudī,* by which we would be able to go toward the Divine Presence.

Maulana, father of three sons and one daughter, liked to draw comparisons from the life of children, or rather from the very beginning of their life in the mother's womb. The sperm loses its individuality to grow into a much higher being, and the embryo— so he repeatedly states—is perfectly happy in its prison of blood. If someone were to tell it that a world of colors and scents, of wide gardens and vast meadows lay outside its dark, warm prison, it would disbelieve him. It is exactly the same with human beings: they are so bound to the world of colors and forms, to the "house of clay and water," that they cannot imagine another world beyond this one, a world of spiritual bliss, of subtlety and beauty beyond description, a world in which the present actions of humanity will become visible just as flowers and grass grow in spring once the winter of the material world has passed away.

When a child is born, his behavior at first is worse than that of an animal; he is unable even to keep clean—and yet God helps him to grow into a beautiful human being. The baby is swaddled and placed in the cradle—and anyone who has seen the narrow cradles in Konya, hanging from the ceiling, will agree with Maulana that only a very small child could feel at ease there (how would a grown person live bound and swaddled in such a small prison?). Thus the moment the spirit grows more mature, it will flee from the bondage of material forms. As for the cradle, it has to be moved gently, and Maulana sometimes sees his heart, longing for the Beloved, being constantly rocked to silence its longing. For in the beginning the baby knows only his mother's milk (just as the lover knows only his beloved's presence) and cries to be fed so that the milk begins to flow—just exactly as the grown lover of

God cries and pleads in the hope that the milk of Divine Kindness may flow from "teats of grace" (a favorite expression in the *Mathnawī*).

The infant can digest only milk; if one tried to feed him bread or meat, he would die. Thus the beginner on the mystical path, or the externalist, should be given very simple spiritual food, because the teaching of higher mysteries would be dangerous for him. Only when the "teeth of reason" have grown sufficiently strong can one offer him more substantial nourishment.

Now comes the time when the child has to enter school, and Maulana Rumi knows very well that children are never particularly fond of going to school. The *Mathnawī* contains a highly naturalistic scene in which a father and mother quarrel over sending their little boy to school. The mother wants the tender child to stay home for a while longer because she pities him, whereas the father insists that he begin his education. The mother symbolizes the *nafs,* the lower soul, the base human qualities that impel us to seek comfort and pleasure at the cost of our spiritual education. The father—in this as in all stories—represents the Intellect, that power which leads human beings toward the right path, instructing them in religious duties and obedience to the God-given law. But the father's order does not preclude the possibility that the child still refuses to go to school: much as Intellect may admonish him, school is not to his liking. Therefore one must cajole him with promises—"I'll buy you a birdie, I'll give you cookies or some pistachio nuts"—to persuade him to obey, just as Divine Wisdom holds the joys of Paradise out to human beings in order to lead them onto the right path. And Maulana does not hesitate to tell the lively story of some naughty boys who all morning long repeat to their teacher that he looks so miserable that he had better go to bed; finally the poor teacher believes it and the triumphant children have a day off—that happens when one imitates others without investigating the situation with one's own reasoning.

However, the school can also serve as a model of life: Maulana knew that an educator has to be patient and slow, and must try to encourage the pupil. And although Maulana himself had been removed from the "normal" way of life and had experienced a rapture unknown to those around him, he was fully aware that normally spiritual education and guidance on the path toward Reality is a long and time-consuming process. In Fīhi mā fīhi he tells of a child learning to write; as he fills his slate with letters, one more shapeless than the next, the teacher points to the one letter that looks approximately correct, praises the child's skill, and encourages him by saying, "This was very good, and look, that one could be a bit better, and over here you just have to change a stroke," and so on. Thus in the course of time the child will learn how to write a decent, perhaps even flawless line. Such is the wisdom of the spiritual guide. The real school, however, the School of Love, is a school of fire in which the pupil is slowly "cooked" and matures. And if the parents first present a doll to their little girl and a wooden sword to their boy to teach them "by metaphors," the time will come when the children will be confronted with reality: the girl will become a mother, the boy a fighter. In the same way, the mysteries of Divine Love cannot be openly told to humankind; one needs symbols and metaphors, stories and "covers." Would a child understand how sweet the union of a loving couple is? No, one has to explain that "it is like sugar. . . ."

Maulana was a child of his time when he depicted women as somewhat deficient in intellect and indulged in a lengthy description in Fīhi mā fīhi of the difficulties of married life: marriage, he claims, serves man to learn patience with the absurdities of women and to put up with their nonsensical talk; by doing so he develops his own virtues, just as if one were rubbing off one's impurities on a towel. Marriage, he concludes, is something for the strong, and therefore Islam has no monkery: to flee from the realities of normal life, to avoid contact with the other sex seemed to him easier than the day-to-day struggle with one's wife. One can interpret the very matter-of-fact description in *Fīhi mā fīhi* as a parable, for in traditional literature woman stands for the *nafs,* the principle of the lower soul, the base instincts, and the duty of the believer is to constantly battle against and educate his *nafs.* This constant battle is the "greater Holy War," as a *ḥadīth* claims. Although Islamic tradition never mentions Eve's share in Adam's fall—a scene that is unknown in the Koranic passage concerning the Fall—yet Maulana, like so many other ascetically minded writers and thinkers of every persuasion in the medieval world, still makes one of his heroes sigh: "First and last my fall was through woman" (M VI 2799).

Woman seems to draw him backward, but—as is implied by the remark about rubbing off one's impurities—such an experience has its advantages as well: in the *Mathnawī* one reads the story of Kharaqani, a famous Persian Sufi of the early eleventh century, whom a disciple once wanted to visit. The visitor encountered only the Sufi's wife at home, who told him in spiteful words what a good-for-nothing, lazy idiot her husband was (one is somewhat reminded of Socrates and his Xanthippe!). The disciple, deeply disappointed, and hurt in his feeling toward the master, proceeded to the forest to overcome his worries. There he saw Kharaqani mounted on a lion, on whose back he had also loaded kindling wood, while a snake served him as a whip. The disciple, greatly astounded, told the master what his wife had said, but the saint only smiled and consoled him: for all the patience he had shown toward his terrible wife, God had recompensed him with such grace that even lions and snakes now served him willingly.

The negative attitude toward women that can be seen in Maulana's work has its origin in the traditional ascetic beliefs prevalent not only in early Sufism but even more sharply in Christian and Buddhist monasticism: woman is the seducer, Satan's instrument. For the Muslims this view—which stands in stark contrast to the Prophet's own words and practice—was facilitated by the fact that the Arabic word *nafs,* which was usually understood as the *nafs ammāra,* "the soul inciting to evil" (Sura 12/53), is grammatically feminine and thus could be associated with any number of images and metaphors. This negative attitude was strengthened by another grammatically feminine word, *dunyā,* "this world," "the world of matter" (as contrasted with *al-ākhira,* the "other world"). Representations of the material world as a dangerous woman occur in Islamic literature as they do in Christian texts as well as in Manichaean and gnostic writings. Thus, "Mistress World," the *Frau Welt* of German poets, appears in Maulana's work as well, and he describes this little old hag, who reeks like a little garlic, in a memorable diatribe (D 2776). In the *Mathnawī,* he goes even more into detail: the old strumpet World tries to entice young men, and to conceal her wrinkles and her hideous face tears apart the beautifully illuminated pages of a Koran and pastes them on her cheeks. The ghastly harlot must be assiduously avoided, for she devours her own children.

However, it would be surprising if Maulana had seen women only in a negative light. His marriages were happy, as far as we can see, and his second wife, Kira Khatun, was a remarkable woman, praised for her deep spirituality. Thus, toward the end of the above-mentioned chapter in *Fīhi mā fīhi* that deals with the challenges of married life, he acknowledges that there is no need to keep good women secluded, because they know what to do and how to behave, while a bad woman will always find a ruse to escape and misbehaves in proportion to the attempt to keep her secluded.

But even more: in the *Mathnawī* (M 1 2433f.), in the midst of commenting upon the Prophet's word that "many a woman prevails over the intelligent," Maulana suddenly turns from the critical approach to a praise of woman:

> She is a ray of God, she is not that "sweetheart"—
> She is a creator, one would almost say: she is not created!

There is no doubt that men and women have to go the same way, and that both must strive to fulfill the duties that the Koran prescribes for believers. For one important aspect of Maulana's teaching is human responsibility. It may be difficult to understand how he was able to combine this emphasis on human responsibility with his firm belief in God's all-embracing power and in God as the sole author of all acts: He creates without secondary causes, and "the whole Koran is the cutting off of secondary causes." However, as the Koran reminds us again and again that every act, nay every thought in this life will become visible in the other world at the Day of Resurrection, Maulana turns to this aspect of the Koranic teaching. Man, he feels, is a camel on which the packsaddle "free will" has been placed, and it is up to him to use this saddle correctly—that is, to load it with obedience and good works, not with the straw and rubbish of harmful and unnecessary actions. For the belief in absolute predestination means to ascribe the responsibility for one's own sins to God.

This point is made quite clear in a story that appears both in a late poem of the *Dīwān* and in *Fīhi mā fīhi*:

> A man entered an orchard, climbed a tree, and ate the fruits. When the gardener discovered him, he claimed to be eating God's fruits with God's permission. The gardener made him descend, called the servants, and gave him a sound thrashing "with the stick of God" until the man confessed that he had stolen the fruits by his own will, not following the Divine will. . . .

In this approach to the problem of free will and predestination, Maulana seems to follow his father's theological stance, but the danger of ascribing one's own sins to God by accepting absolute predestination was also known to other Muslim thinkers, in particular when they dealt with Satan's disobedience. However, Maulana has formulated the secret of free will and its application in a beautiful verse in the *Mathnawī*:

> Free will is the endeavor to thank God for His Beneficence.

> (M 1 929)

But what about the formula *inshā Allāh,* "if God willeth," which is implicitly recommended in the Koran (Sura 68/18)? Does it not incite people to laziness and lack of enterprise? On the contrary, says Maulana, to say "So God willeth," *Deo volente,* does not mean to throw all responsibility upon God, but rather should instigate man to work harder in order to reach ever higher echelons on the spiritual path. One is responsible for one's actions, for as the Prophet says, "This world is the seedbed for the other world"— an adage repeated frequently by Maulana. It is clear for him: "When you plant colocynth, you cannot expect sugarcane!" And thus he admonishes his listeners:

> Eat the fruit that you yourself have planted,
> Dress in the garment that you yourself have spun!

Here is the ancient idea that actions and thoughts constitute, as it were, a garment for one's soul. In both the *Dīwān* and the *Mathnawī,* Maulana teaches his audience the importance of proper actions— sometimes in medical terminology:

> Look at the vial of the urine of actions! (D 1134)

for the physician can easily diagnose the soul's ailments from this "vial," and when "a worm has fallen into one's tooth," one ought to extract the tooth lest its poison permeate the whole body (M V 3181).

One might question Maulana's optimism concerning the "recompense" of one's actions: if the world is only "like the dream of a sleeper," as a tradition claims, how can one's acts bear fruit? But Maulana takes the related words of the Prophet, "People are asleep, and when they die they awaken," and tells his audience that in the morning light of Eternity one will see what one has done in one's dream state, and the dreams will be interpreted properly. Is not this life like winter, when the seed lies under the soil and snow but will bear fruit in the spring, when the sun of eternity shines? Here again Maulana is in full harmony with the Koranic argumentation, for in the Koran resurrection was explained to the unbelieving Meccans through the image of the dead earth that sprouts plants and green shoots when the spring rains quicken it.

But—so predestinarians may object to Maulana's arguments—is not everything ordered and ordained from the beginning of time? Is not everything that will happen and should happen written on the *lauḥ maḥfūẓ,* the Well-Preserved Tablet? There is even a *ḥadīth* to this effect: *qad jaffa'l-qalam,* "The Pen has dried up," that is, what has been written on the Tablet of Destiny cannot be changed. For Maulana, however, this word assumes a different meaning: it means only that it is written that every good action will be recompensed and every evil act will be punished. This one basic truth is inscribed on the Tablet and can never be changed.

Still, Rumi is pragmatic enough to know that every creature can act only in the framework of his, her, or its abilities. Human beings differ like the letters between *A* and *Z,* and therefore their possibilities and capacities are different; hence they will be judged according to how they make use of their capacities.

> One beats the ox because he refuses to carry the yoke,
> One does not beat him because he does not sprout wings!
>
> (M V 3102)

Every human being, like every other creature, has his or her place in the great, wonderful world. Maulana describes the unity that underlies everything in a beautiful image: the world is like a tent, and all of us are needed to make this tent. Everyone's work is his or her praise of God: when the weaver who prepares the fabric does it well in the hope of serving the perfect completion of the tent, he praises God in his way; there is the ropemaker and there are those who fix the ropes, and all strive to perform their duties as well and as carefully as possible. Each one is (or, we may add, should be) happy and content, as all know that they are working for the tent of the lovely King who one day will sit in the center, surrounded by those who serve Him in silence and in love. But this leads to another question: would it not be wonderful if everyone would concentrate exclusively upon his or her duties toward God? Is this not the true goal of Creation? No, says Maulana, and here again he follows his father's argumentation; for if everyone were occupied solely with adoration and worship, the world would not continue. But since God has created the world as a mirror for His beauty, He wants it to continue, and therefore He has blessed many people with negligence so that they are busy with their worldly occupations: they get married, have children, build houses, look after agriculture, or write books. All these things in one way or another also serve the glorification of God or the fulfillment of His will. Maulana makes this quite clear in his advice to the powerful minister Mu'inuddin Parwana, who complained that his constant political occupation and uninterrupted warfare did not allow him to devote himself to the study of God's word or the Prophet's traditions as much as he wished. Maulana replied:

> These works too are work done for God, since they are means to procure peace and security for the realm of the Muslims.

The political activities of the minister by which the Muslim community is protected are as important in God's plan as are devotions and study. Here Rumi seems to develop a working ethic that sounds quite modern and acceptable. He knows that those who are matured on the way to God, or on the path of Love, are like ripe wheat:

> The world is like amber [*kahrubā*, "straw robber"] and
> attracts the straw—
> When the wheat bears fruit, it does not bother about the
> amber [because it can no longer be attracted by it]
>
> (D *Tarji'band* NO. 25)

Maulana admonishes the reader to keep in mind an important saying: "The believer is the believer's mirror." One can see one's own faults better in others, and if one dislikes something in another person, one should first try to purify oneself of that very quality. Is it not so that we do not mind dipping our own hands in a soup pot even though there may be scars or wounds on them, while we shudder when we see others do the same? The constant observation of others in order to learn how to behave is highly important, and the rules of *ṣuḥbat,* "company," have always played a central role in Sufism. Only by using every chance to learn from one's neighbors what may and may not be acceptable can one proceed on the spiritual path.

The goal of the human being in this world is to become a true man, *mard.* The word *man* here stands in contrast to those who are described in the Koran as being "like animals, nay, even more erring" (Sura 7/179). To be sure, "not everyone who has a human face is a human being," as Maulana learned from Sana'i, but he, like all Sufis, dreamt of the Man of God and has described the quest for such a spiritual hero in one of his most famous poems (D 411), which became a kind of motto for modern thinkers such as Muhammad Iqbal in Pakistan. Taking up the story of Diogenes, who went around the town with a lantern in search of a true human being, Rumi has his seeker, who "went around the city last night with a lantern," exclaim:

> I am sick of beasts and animals; my wish is for a human
> being, *insānam ārzūst!*

The use of this image occurs three times in Maulana's work, which shows how important the quest for the "true human being" was. The term *mard,* "man," had long been common to the Persian Sufi poets, and it was customary to consider human beings as classified in three stages, as is expressed in an Arabic saying coined in India at about the time Maulana wrote in Anatolia:

> The seeker of the world is a female,
> The seeker of the other world is a hermaphrodite,
> The seeker of the Lord is a male.

This does not, however, preclude the possibility that a woman may also be a "man" in this sense. The "man of God" has nothing to do with biological gender:

> If one could become a "man" by virtue of beard and
>   testicles,
> Every buck would have sufficient hair and beard! (M V 3345)

Nor has outward asceticism or any outward form to do with the true "man," for, as Maulana says, in an allusion to the pretenders to Sufism:

> If every naked person were a "man,"
> Then garlic would also be a man! (D 1069)

The *mukhannath,* however, the hermaphrodite, appears time and again in Maulana's stories as a model of those unreliable, hypocritical ones who belong neither to this world nor to the other, and he cannot help telling of such a person who met a shepherd and then complained that the buck in his herd had given him a funny look and laughed at him.

Maulana seeks the true devotee, the lover of God, and like Sana'i, he too uses the rhyme *mard-dard,* "man"-"pain," for only through pain, through patient suffering, can the human being grow into a veritable "man." It should, however, be noted that the term *insān-i kāmil,* "the Perfect Man," in the technical sense as used by Ibn 'Arabi and even more by the latter's followers, never occurs in Maulana's work: his ideal man was the one perfected in love and suffering, not someone who had attained a certain stage in a gnostic system.

Once the human being has grown and has tried to fulfill his

duties as well as possible, he is ready for death. Using the traditional contrast of the "white, beautiful, strong Turk" and the "black, ugly, weak Hindu," which was in use since the early eleventh century in Persian writing, he explains that death is indeed the true mirror for everyone: to the lovely Turk it will appear beautiful, to the black person, black. All of life is a preparation for the moment when we throw off our colorful garb to receive the single-colored garment of spirituality, and Maulana has often sung of the beatitude of the state of dying "in the lap of God's grace." He calls his friends to die before the Beloved, to die with a smile like a rose.

It may therefore seem surprising when he also devotes a number of poems to physical death with all its terror and to bodily resurrection as it is described in the Koran. In *Fīhi mā fīhi* he speaks at length of how the individual limbs of man will witness against him in case he denies any of his sins, and among his poems are dramatic visions of the confusion that people will experience on the day when the trumpet is blown. But perhaps his finest poem on individual death is one that utilizes the ancient Iranian idea of the *daena,* the spirit who encounters the dead in the other world and who appears as either a beautiful maiden or an ugly hag, depending upon the soul's former actions, an idea that Rumi cleverly interweaves with Koranic expressions concerning the "faithful Muslim women." Thus he tells the pious listener:

> Your fine ethical qualities will run before you after your
>   death—
> Like moon-faced ladies do these qualities proudly walk. . . .
> When you have divorced the body, you will see *houris* in
>   rows,
> "Muslim ladies, faithful women, devout and repenting
>   ladies" (Sura 66/5)
> Without number will your characteristics run before your
>   bier . . .

In the coffin these pure qualities will become your
companions,
They will cling to you like sons and daughters,
And you will don garments from the warp and woof of your
works of obedience. . . . (D 385)

Thus, each of us will see the results of our works in one way or
another, and it is up to us to do whatever we can to achieve a
happy life thereafter. The elect, however, those who have lost
themselves in God and in Love—will find their own recompense
in eternal flight.

Maulana was not a systematic thinker, and therefore it is not
easy to find out how he imagined the human being and the
relationships between the different parts of body, soul, spirit, and
heart. One thing is clear, however: like his predecessors, Maulana
knows that the human person consists of several layers, beginning
with the body, which consists of the four elements and manifests
the traditional four temperaments. But the body is merely a husk
that surrounds the spirit; it is like a guest house in which new
guests constantly come and go. The outward body essentially is
unimportant for men; were not the Prophet and his uncle Abu
Jahl of the same family, hence similar in appearance? And yet how
vast was the distance between the two! The one was destined to
be the final prophet for humanity; the other remained an accursed
infidel to the very end. This body is rather like a thornbush that
hides the beautiful spirit; or it is like a rope tied to the foot of the
soul. Maulana illustrates this situation by way of the story of the
mouse who fell in love with a frog and tied him by a rope to her
foot; understandably, both perished, as will readily happen if the
body overpowers the spirit. It should therefore be educated by
fasting lest it become too disobedient. Maulana once called the
body "dust on the mirror Spirit"—a dust that hides the radiant
spiritual substance that is found beneath it. Elsewhere he sees it as
a "vessel for the wine Soul," imagery that at least invests the body

with a certain value. For after all, without the body not much can be achieved. In keeping with traditional physiology, Maulana speaks of the five senses, but he is quick to remind the listener that each of the five senses corresponds to an inner sense by which man can understand the higher realities. The senses as they appear to us are like horses; they need an intelligent rider (generally, Reason or Intellect) who can guide them to the right path, direct them on the way of obedience.

A second component of the human being is the *nafs,* the soul, which, understood absolutely, usually refers to the lower instincts or base faculties. However, the *nafs* can be educated, as becomes clear from the three references in the Koran: the *nafs ammāra bi's-sū,* "that which incites to evil" (Sura 12/53); the *nafs lawwāma,* the "blaming soul" (Sura 75/2), which by and large corresponds to our concept of conscience; and finally the stage of *nafs muṭma'inna,* "the soul at peace" (Sura 89/27), the stage from which it can return to its Lord. Maulana, like most Sufi authors, uses the term generally, in an unqualified sense, to represent the lower faculties, and the imagery he uses to describe this dangerous thing is quite colorful: it can be a dog or a wolf, a cow or (often) a woman; it is equated with Pharaoh, since it wants to act as the "highest Lord" (Sura 79/24). Sometimes it is a black Hindu (as contrasting with the white Turk, the higher principle), or a serpent or dragon that can be blinded by the emerald, which represents Love or the spiritual master's glance, conferring his blessing. Rumi's references to the *nafs* are often tempered with humor:

> When the *nafs* says "meow" like the cat,
> I put it in the bag like the cat! (D 1656)

One has, however, to remember that the *nafs,* especially when it appears as a dog or a camel, can be trained: even the *nafs* camel, if it undergoes spiritual education or is suddenly intoxicated by Love, can serve to carry its owner into the presence of the Beloved, and a *kalb mu'allam* (trained dog) can protect its owner and keep the enemy at bay. But such education cannot be achieved by strict discipline and harsh asceticism alone. It is Love that is needed to transform man's "demon" into an angel, his base metal into gold.

Maulana dwells intensely upon the possibility of such a transformation, yet he is aware that constant vigilance is required:

> Once Solomon leaves, the demon becomes the emperor;
> When patience and intellect go, your *nafs* becomes "inciting
>   to evil" (D 455)

And even if the *nafs* does not return to its evil behavior when one does observe it, it has other ruses as well. Maulana knows all too well that even works of obedience can be the result of the *nafs*'s activities, for many people are induced to spiritual pride by works of obedience. Hence:

> The *nafs* has a rosary and a Koran in its right hand
> And a sword and a dagger hidden in its sleeve.
>
> (M III 2554ff.)

On a somewhat different level, however, one should also mention here a saying that is regarded by many as one of the most important words of wisdom in Sufism. That is the alleged *ḥadīth* "*Man 'arafa nafsahu faqad 'arafa rabbahu*": "Who knows himself [or: his *nafs*] knows his Lord." In other words, the one who has discovered the deepest secret of the self has found God in the "ocean of his soul." The word *nafs* is used here in the classical sense of "self," without the negative connotation that it usually carries in mystical texts. Maulana, who quotes this saying several times, invents a beautiful story to explain it that seems to me to reveal much of his own soul: he tells how Ayaz, the Turkish officer at the court of Sultan Mahmud of Ghazna who was the king's favorite, was accused by people of going every morning to a secret chamber where, his adversaries suspected, he had hidden some special treasure. Mahmud sent someone to follow his friend, and

Ayaz was seen entering the room, in which he kept a pair of old, worn-out shoes and a tattered coat. Asked the reason for his daily visit, he replied that these objects reminded him of his previous poverty and destitution and made him grateful each day anew for the bounty he had received from the Sultan. Ayaz then cited the saying "Who knows himself knows his Lord"—explaining that by knowing and realizing his utter poverty, he was able to recognize the boundless greatness and kindness of his master. Maulana sees in Ayaz's attitude a model for the believer: knowing his own destitution, he gratefully acknowledges his Lord's eternal bounty; by recognizing his own limitations, he recognizes the unlimited grace of God. To my knowledge, this is a quite exceptional interpretation of the saying, but one that clearly demonstrates Maulana's deep faith and trust.

Let us return after this little excursion to the next element of which humans are made. Maulana once compared the *nafs* and lust to autumn, to the time when nature begins to die, to enter a state that is frozen and seemingly hopeless, while reason, *'aql,* is compared to spring. This reason, or intellect, is made of light and should be grounded in the Universal Intellect, the *'aql-i kull,* as Maulana sometimes remarks in the more philosophical verses and in *Fīhi mā fīhi.* In fact, the *'aql-i kull* illuminates the horizons, while partial reason "blackens the books of action" (M III 2532), because it may lead to unlawful acts, and this leads to a bad result on Doomsday, when the Books are opened: black books mean sinfulness. In one passage he considers the whole world to be the outward form of Universal Reason (M IV 3259). Normal partial reason gains its strength from there, and it is the solid guide to the door of the Beloved. *'Aql* appears under different guises, as does the *nafs*: it is the prerequisite of religiously valid acts and can therefore be the patient teacher; it is the king's faithful minister, the *mufti* who gives legal opinions, and at times it is also the market superintendent who curbs the destructive activities of the *nafs* when the latter, like a misbehaving villager, causes a riot in the marketplace. Reason is also like the police officer who is able to guide the seeker to the king's gate but is not himself allowed inside. Or else Maulana sees a man on the way to the tailor with a bundle of cloth; Reason shows him the way, but as soon as the tailor has decided how he will cut the cloth, there is nothing further that 'aql can do. For how would it know which pattern the tailor has chosen, and how to cut and stitch a coat or a cloak?

There are degrees of reason. Reason's role in checking the activities of the lower faculties may also be understood from Maulana's comparison of Intellect, even First Intellect, to a cat who ensures that the mice of infidelity do not become too powerful in the country. On the whole, 'aql appears as something useful but pedestrian, a necessary guide and yet something that is not aware of the great mystery of Love, for intellect has to stay back, just as Gabriel had to stay back during the Prophet's night journey. The Prophet was allowed into the sanctuary of Love, while the archangel remained outside: so it is with intellect.

The relation between partial intellect (which can err) and Universal Intellect is not always clear, and as Maulana was no theoretician, he probably never intended to offer his listeners a closed system of relationships. Besides the 'aql he also speaks of the soul, *jān,* "a candle burning with a divine flame," a window toward God. The Prophet, as Maulana sings more than once, is the *jān-i jān,* "the soul of the soul," and he knows, as Sufis before him knew, that the souls of the lovers are basically one. It is only the bodily husk that separates them in time and space; "when the grapes are pressed, the husks disappear and the unity of the wine of the spirit becomes evident" (D 1077).

The body is pregnant with the soul (D 2285), says Maulana in an allusion to Mary and Jesus, and he repeats this idea in the line saying that "the soul is like Christ in the cradle 'outward form' (D 2176). But the soul, lovely child in the cradle "body," is not only a Jesus-like child; it is also the lady who lives in the house of the body, and once it goes away, the time of death has come, as Maulana says in a delightful image:

> When the soul goes, make room for me under the dust—
> Dust gathers in the house when the lady has gone away!
>
> (D 830)

It is difficult if not impossible to draw an exact line between the use Maulana makes of the terms *jān,* "soul," and *rūḥ,* "spirit," the spiritual principle that is given, according to the Koran "by order of my Lord" (Sura 17/85). Thus the relationships between intellect, spirit, soul, and heart are not always clear in Rumi's work and at times are even contradictory.

There is, however, one thing that is absolutely clear: the organ that is dearest to Maulana is the heart, *dil.* He sings of it frequently in tender, moving verses, often using the word *dil* as a recurring rhyme word, and it would be a worthwhile enterprise to collect all the lines in which he describes this heart, now as a timid little darling, now as a being of such power that it can squeeze the heavens like a kerchief, now crying to be rocked in its cradle, now encompassing within itself heaven and earth and their very Creator.

> His love took my painful heart in its palm and smelled it:
> If this heart is not nice, how can it be a nosegay for Him?
>
> (D 2130)

The heart is a house and a garden, it is a mosque, even the *masjid al-aqṣā,* the "farthest mosque" in Jerusalem; it is the Kaaba, the house of God, and it is also the Throne of God on which He seated himself. The little shivering heart, likened to a fish in the frying pan, is also a window through which one can see the Beloved, or it is a glass bottle inhabited by the beloved fairy, the *dulcis hospes animae,* the "sweet guest of the soul," as medieval Christian writers used to call the Divine indwelling in the heart.

But there are two further sets of images that are particularly essential to the understanding of Rumi's thought. According to the first, the heart is a mirror (an idea known to earlier Sufis) that must be polished (it is an age still of metal mirrors!); that is, it has to undergo a long period of hard asceticism. At last the radiant reflection of the Beloved will appear in the mirror, and lover and Beloved will become, as it were, mirrors for each other. The finest description of the constant polishing of the mirror heart is elaborated by Maulana in a story that he found in Ghazzali's *Iḥyā' 'ulūm ad-dīn* and, somewhat later, in Nizami's *Iskandarnāma*. But it shows his ingenuity that he reversed the role of the protagonists and thus tells in the *Mathnawī* how the painters of China and Byzantium undertook a painting contest. In Persian literature, China was *the* country connected with painting, and the skill of Chinese painters was regarded as unsurpassable, especially that of Mani (the founder of Manicheism, who was transformed in Persian imagery into a Master Painter because the Muslims were aware of the lavishly illuminated Manichaean manuscripts). Thus the Chinese produced a stunningly colorful picture on the white marble walls of the palace. But when the Byzantines were asked to show their painting, they drew back the curtain and lo! they had polished the marble wall to such perfection that the Chinese painting was reflected in it and looked even more beautiful than the original. Such polishing is the task of the lover, so that the Divine Beloved may radiate in His full glory within the heart—for what can one offer to Yusuf, the Beloved, but a pure mirror so that He can see His own beauty?

The second major image complex is that related to the purification of the heart, the emptying of the house of all it may still contain. The Sufis—and thus Maulana—use the metaphor of the "sword" or "broom" of *lā*, ("no"), the first word of the profession of faith, *Lā ilāha illā'Llāh*, "There is no deity save God." Like a sword, the *la* cuts off everything that is not God; or else the house must be cleaned by this broom so that the Beloved alone can reside in it. In this context, Maulana's story of the lover and the Beloved has been quoted again and again; in simple words it conveys the necessity of the devotee's annihilation in the Beloved.

> A man knocked at the door of his beloved.
> "Who are you, trusted one?" thus asked the friend.
> He answered: "I!" The friend said: "Go away,
> Here is no place for people raw and crude!"
> What, then, could cook the raw and rescue him
> But separation's fire and exile's flame?
> The poor man went to travel a whole year
> And burned in separation from his friend,
> And he matured, was cooked and burnt, returned
> And carefully approached the friend's abode.
> He walked around it now in cautious fear
> Lest from his lips unfitting words appear.
> His friend called out: "Who is there at my door?"
> The answer: "You, dear, *you* are at the door!"
> He said: "Come in, now that you are all I—
> There is no room in this house for two 'I's!" (M I 3056–63)

Only God has the right to say "I," and the heart must be emptied to receive Him. And Maulana never ceases to marvel at the fact that He who is not contained by heaven and earth can yet dwell within the tiny human heart, that He lovingly descends into our hearts, which are broken for His sake, there to dwell like a treasure in the ruins.

It is in these descriptions of the loving heart that Maulana reaches the heights of poetical imagination, for the heart is more important than all the other elements that together form a human being: the *nafs*, dangerous and yet willing to be tamed by Love; intellect, useful, even indispensable until the goal is almost at hand, but unable to enter the secret chamber of Love; the spirit *rūḥ*, or/ and soul *jān*; and finally the heart, through which the Beloved can be attained by serving as His mirror or His sacred house. But what is one to do when the lover has lost his heart, when the Beloved has carried it away?

> You say: "The house of the king [*khāqān*] is the heart of
> those who are yearning"—
> I have no heart, O my soul! So where would you find your
> house? (D 575)

7

The Koran, the Prophets, and the Saints

Mathnawī-yi maulawī-yi maʿnawī
hast qurʾān dar zabān-i pahlawī.

The spiritual couplets of Maulana
are the Koran in the Persian tongue.

THUS WROTE JAMI in fifteenth-century Herat, the capital of the
Timurid empire in what is now Afghanistan, in the ancestral
country of Maulana. Maulana's biographer Aflaki, who wrote
almost a century after the master's death and a century before
Jami, goes even further: he tells how Husamuddin Chelebi dreamt
that he saw the Prophet with the *Mathnawī* in his hands, reading
from it and praising its author (*Man.* 787).

Western readers of the *Mathnawī* have sometimes wondered at
Jami's statement: this book filled with stories, some strange, others
known from *Kalīlah wa Dimna,* stories reflecting the folk traditions
of the Middle East or retelling legends of the prophets and saints—
what has such a book to do with the sacred scripture of Islam and
its tremendously powerful style, which is considered absolutely
inimitable and, despite its many themes, focuses always on the one
central truth of Islam: faith in the one, unique God, His power,

and His way of acting toward those who serve Him or who disobey Him; it is a book of legal prescriptions as well, a guide to our proper conduct, filled with the promise of grace and the threat of divine wrath.

Yet as one continues to study the *Mathnawī* and, to a certain extent, the *Dīwān,* one is amazed to discover various allusions to Koranic sayings and events, to verses that the non-Muslim who does not know the Book by heart will scarcely recognize but that will ring out to those who have committed it to memory; particularly those who, as a true Sufi should, have "Koranized" their memory and now live and breathe in the words of the revelation.

Like other mystics of Islam, Maulana had immersed himself in the sacred words, and in one of his memorable passages in *Fīhi mā fīhi* he explains what the Koran means to him:

> The Koran is a two-sided brocade. Some enjoy the one side, some the other. Both are true and correct, as God Most High wishes that both groups might have use from it. In the same way, a woman has a husband and a baby; each of them enjoys her in a different way. The child's pleasure comes from her bosom and her milk, that of the husband from kisses and sleeping and embrace. Some people are children on the path and drink milk—these enjoy the external meaning of the Koran. But those who are true men know of another enjoyment and have a different understanding of the inner meanings of the Koran.

This explanation is typical of Rumi: everything has its *ẓāhir* and its *bāṭin,* its external and its internal meaning, just as every limb of the human body corresponds to a spiritual limb. Still, it must be emphasized that Rumi is not a thorough *bāṭinī* who would deny the importance of the external meaning of the revelation and look exclusively to the esoteric side; rather, he knows that behind each and every word is hidden a deeper wisdom that only those who have eyes to see can understand. This knowledge enables him to insert Koranic quotations into his poetry in places where one would barely expect them, and his son, Sultan Walad, following some deprecating remarks about those who study the famous literary works of Anwari and other classical Persian poets, writes:

> The poetry of God's friends is all explanation of the mysteries of the Koran, for they are annihilated from themselves and exist through God. (VN 212f.)

Those who have reached complete annihilation in the Divine Beloved have bound their souls, as it were, to the eternal root of everything, and when they speak, their words are inspired by the divine words and become understandable also to those who do not know the language in which they are spoken: the spirit of divine inspiration can be grasped even by those who do not understand the outward words (Maulana gives a good example of this truth when he speaks of his Greek listeners, who, without knowing Persian, yet were moved to tears by his words).

His utter proximity to the Divine Word makes it easy for Maulana to insert words and phrases from the Koran into his poetry—the lyrical as well as the didactic—without distorting the metrical pattern of a poem. A particularly fine example is number 1948 in the *Dīwān,* where one finds a Koranic saying in almost every hemistich, making a total of twenty quotations. In a poem (D 2538) with the pen name Salahuddin, the Koranic phrase "Praised be He who traveled by night [with His servant]" (*sub-ḥāna'lladhī asrā,* Sura 17/1) occurs even as a recurring rhyme. Indeed, it would be useful to read Maulana's poetry as a kind of *tafsīr,* a commentary on the Koran, and to reconstruct his interpretations from the numerous quotations. It is remarkable, however, that one of the favorite verses of most Sufis actually does not often appear (at least not in its exact wording). This is Sura 2/257: "Whithersoever you turn there is the Face of God." Perhaps the truth of this word was so evident to Maulana that he barely deemed it necessary to repeat it, for his whole work could be considered an interpretation of the omnipresence of the Divine Beloved, the Eternal Sun. In *Fīhi mā fīhi* he repeats constantly the statement of Sura 15/27 that "the treasures of heaven and earth are with God," and he comes back time and again (especially in the *Mathnawī*) to God's address to the Prophet in Sura 8/17: "You did not cast when you cast, but God cast." This points to the divine activity that needs no secondary causes: it was God who moved the Prophet's hand during the decisive battle of Badr in 624, when Muhammad hurled sand at the Meccan infidels and thus secured the first Muslim victory.

Maulana also alludes to various customs connected with reciting and learning the Koran. In his time, the custom of reciting *Sura Yāsīn* (Sura 36) for the dead was apparently well known, for he says:

> They say: "Recite *Yāsīn* so that Love will be calmed!"
> What's the use of *Yāsīn* for a soul that has come to the lip
>   [i.e., for someone who is on the point of dying] (D 2609)

He also speaks of the technique of learning the Koran by rote when the child begins with the shortest of the 114 Suras of the Koran, those that are generally used in ritual prayer, and then slowly proceeds backward through at least one or two, if not all thirty, sections of the Holy Book:

> Why are you still reading *'abasa* ["He frowned," Sura 80/1]
> When the child Soul has already reached *tabāraka*, "Blessed
>   be" [Sura 67/1]? (D 2625)

In other words, grief, as it is expressed in the divine address to the Prophet, who was censured when he frowned at the entrance of a blind man, has given way to the joy expressed by the first word of blessing in the preceding section: "Blessed be He in whose hand the kingdom is . . ."

Like most poets of the Islamic world, especially in Iran and the countries under its cultural influence, Maulana used the figures of the Koranic prophets as models for certain types of behavior, as ciphers for general human attitudes. Adam, the first human being, the one before whom the angels prostrated themselves, is the father of humankind, and although he fell because of Satan's ruse (a mistake that did *not* result in an "original sin"), yet he was the first prophet in the long centuries and millennia during which God never left mankind without proper prophetic guidance. He thus is the model for humanity in general. Noah (Nūḥ in Arabic) appears rarely in the lyrical poetry, but in the *Mathnawī* (M II) a lengthy chapter is devoted to him and to the restive son who drowned during the Flood as a consequence of his impatience and disobedience.

Far more important is Ibrahim, the builder of the Kaaba, who, obedient to the divine order, was ready even to sacrifice his son Ishmael (Isma'il), and who entered Nimrod's pyre without fear, whereupon God made the fire "cool and pleasant" for him, as Sura 21/69 tells us. Ibrahim, the monotheist par excellence with his absolute submission to the will of God, is the model for the true believer for whom even fire will turn into a rose garden. His willingness to sacrifice his son (Rumi in one passage even speaks of Isaac (Ishaq), not Ishmael; he was well aware of the Judeo-Christian tradition) fits well into Maulana's conviction that life is made possible only when one lovingly sacrifices one part of one's self after the other. Thus the figure of Ibrahim looms large in Maulana's verse. His favorite prophet, however, is Joseph, or Yusuf, the paragon of beauty, the lost son who returned in glory to heal his blind father's eyes by the fragrance of his shirt; Yusuf, who had to leave home and travel through depths and heights and was honored after being cast down. It seems possible, as I have shown elsewhere, that Yusuf in many instances may represent the Beloved and especially Shams-i Tabriz. Had Shams not disappeared and left Rumi in a state of suffering? Was it not the fragrance of his presence, or rather that of his words, that enlivened the poet? Maulana seems at times to have felt like the lovesick Zulaykha, whose friends cut their fingers without being aware of it when they gazed at Yusuf (Sura 12/31). How can the true lover feel any pain when he beholds his beloved? The key passage that, according to my understanding, reveals the use of Yusuf as cipher for Shams is found at the end of the *Mathnawī*. After admonishing young Husamuddin, in the very beginning of the *Mathnawī,* to "listen to the contents of the tales" and claiming that it will be better to tell of the friend in the stories of others, he turns at the very end of the *Mathnawī* to Zulaykha, describing her state in an unforgettable passage:

> And when she said: The wax is melting softly!
> That was to say: My friend was kind to me.
> And when she said: Look, how the moon is rising!
> And when she said: The willow is now green!
> And when she said: The leaves there are a-trembling,
> And when she said: How nicely burns the rue! . . .
> And when she said: The birds sang to the roses,
> And when she said: Beat firmly all my rugs!
> And when she said: The bread is all unsalted!
> And when she said: The spheres are going wrong. . . .
> She offered praise—that meant, "His sweet embrace,"
> She spoke in blame—that meant, "He's far away!"
> And when she heaped one name upon another—
> Her sole intention was but Yusuf's name. . . .

Whatever Zulaykha saw, she discovered Yusuf in it, and it was his name that served her as a fur coat in the dead of winter and was food in times of hunger. Is not the entire net of stories that Maulana wove together in the *Mathnawī* to hide the name of his erstwhile beloved like Zulaykha's attempt to hide Yusuf's name in every sentence she says? Similarly, the whole fabric of names that the God-loving mystic repeats is nothing but a veil behind which the One Reality is hidden.

If Yusuf is the Beloved par excellence, the one who radiates Divine Beauty, then Moses is the representative of the *jalāl* side of the Divine, the stern lawgiver-prophet who—as Maulana tells in the delightful story of his encounter with the simple shepherd (see page 168)—has to learn that God can be found also in ways unknown to the lawbound preacher. But Moses is also the man noted for his miracles: his rod became a serpent to swallow the magician's snakes in order to prove his superiority before the arrogant Pharaoh. It was Moses who experienced the manifestation of Divine Glory through the Burning Bush, the recipient of the Divine Light that shone, for Maulana, through the person of Shamsuddin.

Contrasted with Moses, the stern lawgiver, is Jesus, the loving prophet, loved from earliest times by the Sufis, who found in him a model of modesty, charity, and Divine Love. Maulana juxtaposes him and his cousin, the ascetic John the Baptist, who always looks fearful and dour. John—so tells Maulana in *Fīhi mā fīhi*—reprimanded Jesus for his constant smile, asking whether he never thought of God's wrath, while Jesus, again with a smile, asked him in return whether he never thought of God's Loving-kindness. A saint who overheard the conversation then wanted to know from God which of the two He loved more, and the Lord replied: "The one who thinks better of Me!"

Jesus, praised in the Koran as the one who was created through the breath of God, who was granted the gift of speaking in the cradle to attest to his mother's purity, and who was able to give life to clay birds by dint of his breath, just as he could heal the sick by this same breath—Jesus is a wonderful symbol of the beloved whose breath and, even more, whose kiss can quicken the dead or half-dead lover, and whose gentleness and kindness are revealed everywhere. Jesus is pure spirit, and in this context he is usually juxtaposed with his donkey. To be sure, he rode a donkey out of modesty, but the donkey itself, the typical representative of the world of matter and sensuality, in fact has nothing to do with Jesus. The numerous stories related in both the *Dīwān* and the *Mathnawī* in which the donkey is "lost" can be interpreted as pointing to the loss of the material body or to the renunciation, whether voluntary or not, of the world of matter.

Gone the donkey, gone the donkey, gone is he!

Thus sing the Sufis, dancing and clapping their hands, after selling a traveler's donkey in order to get some money to give a joyous musical party. Although Maulana tells the story for a different purpose (i.e., to show the futility of imitating other people's behavior), yet we may well conclude that the loss of the beast is certainly a blessing for its owners, who can now indulge in pure spiritual joy.

As for Jesus, he went to heaven while his donkey stayed on earth. He was not crucified, the Koran states (Sura 4/151), but was taken up to live in the Fourth Heaven. According to Sufi tradition this place was assigned to him because he was carrying a needle with him; otherwise his rank would have been even higher. But for someone completely spiritualized, as Jesus was, even a small needle is a burden as heavy as the treasures of the miserly Qarun, who was swallowed up by the earth.

Maulana, who often alludes in the *Dīwān* to the life-bestowing breath of Jesus, tells a moving story in *Fīhi mā fīhi* about Christ's homelessness: he was not even allowed to stay in a jackal's den but had to wander without shelter through woods and deserts, thrust into homelessness by the Beloved, who hunted him with His love. Thus he was blessed more than if he had found shelter, for it is the constant search for the Beloved, the restless wandering without any visible sign from God, that the spirit "Jesus" must take upon itself to reach perfection. Even more important: when Maulana speaks of pain, he tells the story of Mary, the lovely virgin who in her labor pangs came to a dried-up palm tree; when she clung to its trunk, it showered sweet dates over her (Sura 19/23f.). It was pain that led her to the tree and caused the barren plant to give forth fruit, and Rumi continues:

> The body is like Mary. Each of us has a Jesus, but so long as no pain appears, our Jesus is not born. If pain never comes, our Jesus goes back to his place of origin on the same secret path he had come, and we remain behind, deprived and without a share of him.

Here is the mystical idea of the birth of Christ in the soul that would be expressed half a century later by Meister Eckhart in Germany: the spiritual being will be born in the human soul, provided one willingly takes upon oneself the burden and pain caused by Divine Love.

> Grief for Him is in the heart like a treasure; my heart is
>   "light upon light" [Sura 24/35]
> Like the lovely Mary, who carried Jesus in her womb. (D 565)

And in another verse Maulana sings:

> The soul is like Christ in the cradle "Body."
> Where is the Mary that fashions our cradle? (D 2176)

The donkey, however, has nothing to do with spiritual Jesus:

> Far be the donkey's tail from Jesus's cradle! (D 1107)

For those who "kiss the ass's arse will not enjoy the sweet breath of Jesus" (D 96), as Maulana says with one of his very outspoken descriptions of the contrast of matter and spirit. The infant Jesus, on the other hand, blossoms like a lovely fragrant flower from his mother, who is innocent like a young twig, caressed by the breeze, the breath of the Merciful.

All the stories of the prophets mentioned in the Koran culminate in the "Seal of prophets," Muhammad, whom Rumi often refers to by two of his epithets: Mustafa, "the Chosen One," and Ahmad, "Highly Praised." Muhammad's religion, so says Rumi, is still fresh and healthy after six hundred and fifty years (D 490), and Aflaki's *Manāqib al-'ārifīn* contains many stories that speak of dream appearances of the Prophet to Maulana or members of his family. Despite his deep devotion to Jesus and Mary, Rumi was critical of many Christian customs and of the Christian theological position. Thus in the first book of the *Mathnawī* he tells a revealing story: a ruthless minister invents a ruse to exterminate the Christians without himself becoming involved in bloodshed. He poses as a deeply pious Christian ascetic and after many years calls the leaders of the different Christian sects together to hand each one a document investing the recipient as the ascetic's true successor. However, the statements and orders contained in each of the scrolls completely contradict those in the other documents. After the false ascetic's death the scrolls are opened, and the twelve leaders and their groups begin to fight among themselves, each one claiming to possess the correct version of the Christian doctrine. Only one group remains apart, and its members begin to study the Bible with great care. There they find the name of Ahmad and become Muslims *avant la lettre.*

Maulana alludes here to the famous Muslim interpretation of the word *parakletos* in the Bible, which was understood by the Muslims as a wrong spelling of *perikleitos,* "the highly praised one," in Arabic *aḥmad.* The promise in the Koran (Sura 61/5) that "a highly praised one [Ahmad]" would be sent was seen as the fulfillment of this biblical remark, and as the names Ahmad and Muhammad are derived from the same Arabic root, *ḥ.m.d.,* "to praise," the equation was easily made: Muhammad is the consoler whose coming was predicted in the Christian scripture.

For Maulana, the person of Muhammad stands head and shoulders over every other prophet. He is the "helper of the two worlds" (M III 3132), the one who was the goal and meaning of all earlier religions. Maulana's love of Muhammad was further strengthened by Shams, whom he addresses as "the heir of the Prophet" (D 2473), and a story told by Aflaki reveals the depth of Shams's faith in the Prophet. According to Aflaki, Shams said that

> God Himself cannot do without Muhammad. For He has said in the Koran: "If We wanted We would have sent a messenger to every village" [Sura 25/50]—but He did not want that, and He did not want this *lau shi'nā*, If We had wanted. . . . (*Man.* 665)

It is Muhammad "in whom the whole world will get lost," as his nurse Halima was told when she was worried because the child had been lost (M IV 976). It is the miracle-working Muhammad, whose finger can easily split the moon (cf. Sura 54/1), and those who participate in the eternal light that shines through him can do likewise. But, in any case, the moon felt ashamed of its own face before the more than moonlike beauty of the Prophet, who had lost himself in God and, as Maulana holds, was "a window through which one sees the Creator" (M VI 3197). Hence Maulana's frequent allusions to and direct citations of the verse "You did not cast when you cast" (Sura 8/17), affirming that the Prophet was the instrument through which God worked.

But Muhammad was also the goal and end of the creation. *Laulāka, laulāka mā khalaqtu'l aflāka,* "But for thee, but for thee I would not have created the spheres": thus spoke the Lord in an extra-Koranic saying. And yet, Maulana knew also the sigh of the Prophet: "Wish that the Lord of Muhammad had not created Muhammad!"—a sigh that may sound absurd if one considers the Prophet's role in his life and afterlife; but, as Maulana explains in *Fīhi mā fīhi,* compared with the undivided unity with God that the Prophet enjoyed before his creation, this present life—despite the knowledge that he was an instrument of God—was still a life of separation from which he hoped to return, as the reed longs for its reed-bed home. Even more: in the *Mathnawī* (V 3535ff.) Maulana relates that at some point early in his career as prophet, Muhammad intended to hurl himself from the cave in Mount Hira where he received the first revelations, so heavy seemed the burden of prophethood to him.

A central event in the Prophet's life is his *mi'rāj*, his night journey into the Divine Presence (which was to become the model of the spiritual journey for the Sufis). Here, in the immediate presence of God, where even Gabriel has no access, Muhammad experienced the *waqt*, the "time with God," which for him and all who follow his path is the highest bliss. In this moment God entrusted seventy thousand mysteries to him (Man. 599), and, as Aflaki tells proudly, he saw an effigy of Maulana on the Divine Throne (Man. 365). We need not take the claim seriously; similar remarks are known concerning other celebrated Sufi leaders. What is significant is that Muhammad, in his quality of prophet, had to return to the world to preach what he had learned during this moment of highest bliss. But one should be aware that the "heavenly journey" has nothing to do with spatial relationship. Recalling that Muhammad once warned his followers not to exalt him above Jonah, Maulana elaborates this saying: Jonah's meeting with the Lord was in the belly of the whale, in the darkest depths, while that of the Prophet was in the heights, in full light. Here one is reminded of the two ways of the seeker, the way upward and the way downward, into one's own soul, corresponding roughly to the way of the prophet, who makes things evident in the light of history, and that of the mystic, who finds God "in the ocean of his soul."

> My soul is in heaven, and his [Jonah's] journey is toward the
>   slope—
> because the proximity to God is beyond counting.

Thus says Muhammad in the *Mathnawī* (M III 4512).

Muhammad partakes in the Divine Light; he is a luminous figure. Legend states that he did not cast a shadow, and the arrival of the "light of Muhammad among the infidels is like the coming of the sun unto the dark night." It is this light that manifested itself through Shamsuddin, as we know from the last line of the *Na't-i sharīf,* the eulogy to the Prophet by which the mystical dance is always opened. In this poem,

Yā ḥabīb Allāh rasūl Allāh ki yaktā'ī tū-ī,

the Prophet is surrounded by the tenderest names:

> O friend of God, Messenger of God, you who are unique,
> The one elected by the Mighty One, you are pure and
> without peer.

He is addressed as "light of the eyes of the prophets, cypress in the garden of prophethood, springtime of gnosis, rosebud of the meadow of the Divine Law" as well as the "lofty nightingale," and in the last line Shams is referred to as the one "who knows the mysteries of the Prophet."

Maulana was familiar with an extra-Koranic divine saying that seems to have circulated among the Sufis of Iran and the eastern Muslim world in the late twelfth century, that is, *Anā Aḥmad bilā mīm,* "I am Ahmad without the *m*," that is, *aḥad,* "One." This pun on the letter *mīm,* which was to become a favorite with later Sufis of the eastern (and only eastern!) Muslim world, serves Maulana to show that every addition to perfection is imperfection: the *mīm* is the letter of humanity, and only if it is taken away will the One remain as He was and ever will be. (It is, incidentally, worthy of mention that Maulana used this pun in a discussion with Mu'inuddin Parwana, the powerful minister.)

Among the Koranic references to the Prophet, Maulana seems to have been particularly fond of the Prophet's designation as *ummī* (Sura 7/156, 158). Probably this word originally meant "the one sent to the gentiles," *umma,* but was soon interpreted as meaning "illiterate." For in order to preserve the purity of the Divine Revelation the Prophet had to be illiterate: his knowledge was not acquired by study but rather was poured into him as into a vessel. Speaking on one occasion of those who think that the Koran is not God's word but Muhammad's, Maulana shows that "although it came from Muhammad's lips it was a Divine Word," for when the Prophet had completely lost himself in God, the revelation came through him undetermined by his own words or thought. But he had to be "transported out of himself" so that this miracle could happen. That is why Maulana uses a beautiful image to describe the Prophet's activity: "God was the cupbearer . . . and Muhammad was the goblet full of wine" (D 113), the goblet through which the wine of revelation was poured for mankind.

Elsewhere, in *Fīhi mā fīhi*, Rumi has a more theoretical interpretation of the term *ummī:* the Prophet's knowledge is innate, not acquired, for he takes his knowledge from the First Intellect, the source of all wisdom.

> A hundred thousand books of poetry existed—
> before the word of the illiterate [Prophet] they were put to
> shame! (M I 529)

He who inscribes characters on the face of the moon—how is he to be likened to a simple illiterate person? And his close connection with the source of inspiration, which in more theoretical passages is called the First Intellect, leads Maulana at times to equate Muhammad himself with the First Intellect. And yet where are First Soul and First Intellect compared with him?

> O princely rider of the order "Say!" [*qul*]
> O you, before whose intellect the Universal Soul is like a
> child who out of childishness and ignorance gnaws on its
> sleeve . . . (D 1793)

Thus does Rumi in the *Dīwān* address the Prophet, that one who, according to some poems, is the same as Love. Allusions to the Prophet in the *Dīwān* are otherwise comparatively rare, or at least covert. One finds, however, references to various legends that were woven around him in the course of time. There is the lovely legend of the *hannāna*, the palm trunk that he used in the early days of his preaching to support himself while speaking. When a real pulpit was erected and the palm trunk was thrown out, the poor abandoned thing began to weep and sigh, for it missed the Prophet's touch. Should the human heart be any less loving than a seemingly dead piece of wood? How can a philosopher who denies this miracle find his way to the saints? (M I 3280).

The *Mathnawī*, on the other hand, tells a number of stories about the Prophet, how he spoke to his young wife 'A'isha when the blind man came to visit him, or how he was censured for his unfriendly behavior in *Sura 'Abasa,* "He frowned" (Sura 80/1); still more frequent are tales about his wisdom (how he selected a young leader for the army) and about his kindness. The most typical of these stories is that of the infidel who came to visit him and "ate with seven stomachs" (as infidels use to do); at night he sullied the guest room and ran off, but when he returned in hopes of retrieving a little idol that he had left behind in his haste, he found the Prophet himself cleaning the dirty room and washing the linens (M V 64ff.). Muhammad is also described as visiting the sick (M II 2141ff.), and his kindness is like rain, for he was sent as "mercy for the worlds" (Sura 21/107).

> The fortune of the dervishes has come from "Mercy" [for
>   the worlds];
> Their gowns radiant like the moon, with shawls fragrant like
>   roses! (D 2)

Thinking of these qualities, one wonders why Maulana in *Fīhi mā fīhi* mentions several times the Prophet's saying "I laugh when killing." However, according to Rumi the meaning is that Muhammad had no enemies to kill, and therefore he laughed. Indeed, he is the intercessor for believers, "the boat in the ocean of the

Universe" (M IV 3358). His light impregnates everything it touches; even his handkerchief does not burn in the oven, and he acts as a veritable *kīmīyā,* the philosopher's stone that transforms the copper of human existence into gold (M IV 990), even as he was able to transform his own lower self, his little personal *shaytān,* "demon," into a good Muslim who does only what he is ordered to do—a favorite story of the Sufis, who in the Prophet's word *aslama shaytānī,* "My Satan has become a Muslim" [or: "has completely surrendered"], found the secret of the transformation of man's lower qualities into higher spiritual faculties.

We need not dwell upon the numerous legends and tales concerning the Prophet that Aflaki tells. Even the story of Abu Hurayra's cat, who saved the Prophet's life by killing a snake, is put into Maulana's mouth, culminating in a well-known *hadīth: ta'ashshaqū wa lau bi'l-hirra,* "Love, and be it a cat." Abu Hurayra, incidentally, appears (quite frequently) in the *Dīwān* along with the bag in which he kept his cat; he is a favorite figure from among those of the Prophet's entourage who have been transformed into symbols of faithfulness and friendliness. For it is natural for Maulana, like almost every mystical Muslim writer, to have drawn examples also from those who surrounded the Prophet—be they negative images, such as that of Abu Lahab, "the Father of the Flame" (Sura 111), who according to Maulana was the only one to be deprived of the flame of Divine Love; or positive ones, such as the Prophet's first successor, Abu Bakr, the *yar-i ghar,* "the friend in the cave," who spent the night of the Prophet's emigration to Medina with him in the cave that was mysteriously protected by a spider who wove its web over the entrance. The stern and mighty caliph 'Omar also appears, but more prominently in *Fīhi mā fīhi,* where he is the model of absolute faith, than in lyrical verse. It is understandable that 'Ali, the fourth caliph and husband of Muhammad's daughter Fatima, appears now and then, although not as frequently as one might expect, while his cousin Ja'far at-Tayyār, "the flyer," killed in battle in 630, is often praised as a true hero of loving faith who "flew to Paradise." In a strange verse Shams-i Tabriz is compared to Murtada 'Ali, the first imam of the Shia, while Maulana feels like 'Ali's two martyred sons: like Husayn, who wallowed in his own blood, and like Hasan, who drank poison (D 1944).

The Prophet, however, seems to be present wherever Shams appears:

> If you want the perfect color and fragrance of Ahmadian
> wine,
> O caravan leader, stop for a moment at the gate of Tabriz!
>
> (D 1966)

Muhammad is the last of the God-sent messengers, the "true seal" (M VI 165–72) who opens locks not yet opened with the hand of *Innā fataḥnā*, "Verily We have opened" (Sura 48/1), that is, the one who acts through God and is promised the final victory. However, there are others in the world who continue to teach people on a different level. Never to be compared to the Prophet and yet ever-present among the children of this world, they are sent to diagnose the illnesses of the soul and like beacon lights to guide people to higher levels.

These are the saints, *auliyā'* (sing. *walī*), "the friends [of God]" who "have not fear nor are they sad" (Sura 10/62). The Sufis had begun to develop a complicated hierarchy of saintship around the year 900, culminating in the figure of the *quṭb,* the "Pole" or "Axis" around which the entire firmament of greater and lesser *auliyā'* revolves. For the Sufi, the saint par excellence is manifested in his spiritual master, and it is worthy of mention that Rumi's descriptions of the saints and the *shaykh* or *pir*, the spiritual guide, are found exclusively in the *Mathnawī* and in *Fīhi mā fīhi*. For himself, the ideal "friend of God" was, without any doubt, Shams-i Tabriz, yet Rumi never tried—at least not in a technical sense—to place him into the hierarchy by declaring him the *quṭb*. Shams is a *qalandar*, and *qalandar*, according to the traditional use of the term, were dervishes who roamed about freely and cared little for the externals of Islam. In fact, the word *qalandar* could be used among the official ranks of Sufis as a rather deprecating expression. For Maulana, however, the *qalandar* is the one who has fully realized his union with God and who is happiest immersed in the consuming fire of Divine Love; he is, as Maulana says in a rhyming pun, like the *samandar*, the salamander, which according to ancient belief is so cold that it lives comfortably in the fire. A true *samandar*-like *qalandar*, however, is as difficult to find as the philosopher's stone or the mysterious bird Simurgh. That is how Shams appeared to Maulana: having reached the rank of the Beloved, he could not be enclosed in any traditional scheme, for like a wild lion he would leap out of the fetters of words and thoughts.

It seems natural that Maulana often refers to the great Sufi masters of yore such as Bayezid Bistami (d. c. 874), known for his exclamation *Subḥanī*, "Praise be to me! How great is my majesty!" And the *Mathnawī* tells how the disciples who tried to kill Bayezid for his outrageous claims found themselves stabbing not him but their own bodies; for the saint is a perfect mirror of those around him. Having lost his ego, he reflects the thoughts and wishes of others and reads their thought. In another story, Bayezid appears as the model of strong faith, the perfect Muslim. A story taken over in our century by Muhammad Iqbal in his epic poem *Jāvīdnāma* (1932) tells how a Zoroastrian was invited to embrace Islam but refused, for he felt himself not strong enough to follow the religion represented by the extremely powerful and heroic Bayezid: Islam, he concluded, is not for the weak (M V 3358ff).

A favorite of Sufi writers was Ibrahim ibn Adham, the early ascetic of Balkh, Maulana's home province. He appears in the *Mathnawī,* as he does in general hagiographies, as the prince who,

like the Buddha, went from home into homelessness. Maulana tells
how one night the prince heard strange noises. Upon investigation,
he discovered on the palace roof a group of people who claimed
to be searching for their lost camel. When Ibrahim objected to
such a nonsensical claim, he was told that it was even more absurd
to seek a spiritual life while living in a palace and enjoying the
world, and as he heard that, *Balkh talkh shud,* "Balkh became bitter
for him." (The two words *Balkh* and *talkh* [bitter] are distinguished
in Persian only by the position of their dots.) Thus, Ibrahim is the
model of those who repent. Dhu'n-Nun the Egyptian appears in a
story full of miracles, and I have already mentioned the anecdote
about Kharaqani, whose patience with his intolerable wife was
recompensed (see page 96). A long part of the third book of the
Mathnawī is devoted to Daquqi, an otherwise not-so-prominent
mystic whose visionary power and prayer Maulana describes in a
series of passages that might well deserve a psychologist's attention
(just as all of Maulana's descriptions of and allusions to actual
visionary experience would be worthy of deeper study).

But among all the names that appear more or less openly in
Rumi's stories and allusions, one figure stands out, all the more so
as he is not merely the subject of an anecdote or a legend but is
used repeatedly as a poetical symbol to represent the true lover of
God. This is al-Husayn ibn Mansur al-Hallaj, usually called simply
by his father's name, Mansur, "the victorious one."

Hallaj, who is famed for his statement *"Anā'l-ḥaqq,"* "I am the
creative Truth" (or, as it was soon interpreted to mean, "I am
God"), was cruelly executed in Baghdad on 26 March 922. His
name became a symbol for the suffering lover of God, and later
also for those who claimed the essential unity of all Being;
intoxicated with the wine of Divine Love, Hallaj divulged the
secret of the essential Unity of Being, or also of the loving union
between creature and Creator. So, at least, have his admirers and
critics interpreted his word to this day. Maulana was very fond of
Hallaj, and it is said that he consoled his disciples shortly before

his death with a reference to Hallaj's appearance in spirit to 'Attar, whom he "initiated" into the Sufi path (and indeed, 'Attar's description of Hallaj's death in his *Tadhkirat al-auliyā'* [Biographies of the Saints] became the standard version of the account of the mystic's suffering and death). Maulana said:

> As the spirit of Mansur appeared one hundred and fifty years after his death to the *shaykh* Fariduddin 'Attar and became the *shaykh*'s spiritual guide and teacher, so, too, do you always be with me whatever may happen, and remember me, so that I may show myself to you in whatever form that may be.

Maulana's lyrics abound with images like "Mansur's wine," and he goes so far as to claim that everyone else has drunk a mere cupful of the wine of *anā Allāh* and *anā'l-ḥaqq* respectively, while he has quaffed this wine by the bottle and the vat, so intoxicated is he with love.

He knew, however, that Hallaj and Bayezid had both been "lovers" and had to suffer thereby for their utterances, whereas he himself, being a "beloved," was safe—or so, at least, Aflaki (*Man.* I 466) and, preceding him, Sipahsalar tell us in reference to Sultan Walad's question of why his father, who had uttered even more daring words than these two mystics, was never persecuted.

> How many a lordly Simurgh whose litany was "*Anā'l-ḥaqq*"
> burned his wings and feathers when he flew to that side!
>
> (D 1854)

But what, then, was the difference between Hallaj's "*Anā'l-ḥaqq*" and Pharaoh's claim, "*Anā rabbukum al-a'lā*," "I am your highest Lord" (Sura 79/24)? Hallaj himself had compared his situation to that of Pharaoh and Satan, both of whom dared to use the word *ana* ("I"), Satan saying before the newly created Adam, "I am better than he" (Sura 38/77). Taking up this story (which Hallaj tells in his *Kitāb aṭ-ṭawāsīn*), Rumi states that Hallaj's word is light, whereas Pharaoh's claim was tyranny:

> The "I" of Mansur surely became grace;
>
> That of Pharaoh became a curse, look!

The same argumentation is taken up, years later, in the fifth book of the *Mathnawī*. During those years—that is, between 1262 and 1270 approximately—Maulana explained the *anā'l-ḥaqq* several times in his conversations:

> Take the famous utterance "I am the Divine Truth." Some people consider it a great pretension. But "*Anā'l-ḥaqq*" is in fact great humility. . . . He has annihilated himself and given himself to the winds. He says, "I am the Divine Truth," that is, "I am not, He is all, nothing exists but God, I am pure not-being, I am nothing. . . ."

And in another passage of *Fīhi mā fīhi* he states:

> So, when Mansur's friendship with God reached its utmost
>   goal,
>
> he became an enemy of himself and annihilated himself. . . .

"Like the moth in the candle," we might add, drawing on the metaphor that Hallaj first used in his *Kitāb aṭ-ṭawāsīn*.

Yet Maulana also explains the famous utterance in a different way: he speaks of pieces of cloth that fall into the dyeing vat "He" and thereby experience the *ṣibghat Allāh* (Sura 2/138), the "dyeing of God," in which all colors disappear and only the radiant white remains, whereupon they sing joyfully, "I am the vat." He goes on to compare the mystic to the bar of iron which, heated in the fire, becomes red and fiery until it finally exclaims, "I am the fire." Indeed, its form and outward appearance are that of fire, but substantial union is not achieved: the fire remains fire; the iron, iron. (This same imagery appears both in Christological discussion about Christ's nature and in the writings of mystics in East and West.)

Maulana describes the heavenly feast of union, when the sun dances and claps his hands on the sky while the atoms play like lovers; fountains are intoxicated and roses smile—then the spirit becomes Mansur and calls out "Anā'l-ḥaqq." Similarly, whoever prostrates himself before Shams, whose divine radiance transforms the world, will say "Anā'l-ḥaqq" if the Beloved accepts him. Husamuddin, too, as cupbearer quickens the soul with the morning libation of "Mansuri wine." This is the wine of spiritual love and self-negation, of absolute surrender and the happiness that results from this surrender.

In harmony with almost all Sufi poets in the Persianate tradition, Maulana often speaks of the gallows on which the martyr-mystic Hallaj was executed. The gallows represents good tidings, that is, the promise of union, which can be achieved only through death. Lovers who suffer on the gallows are those who, in the words of the Koran, are "killed but . . . in reality, alive" (Sura 3/169).

The Sufis often asked why Hallaj was put to death, as it was not he who spoke but rather God who made him His instrument, just as He had once spoken through the Burning Bush. But Maulana, though alluding to this idea, is sure that this cruel death was a necessary prerequisite for true life. Is not Hallaj like a ripe apple hanging on the gallows-tree? People throw stones at the apple, but it replies with mute eloquence:

> I am Mansur, hanging from the branch of the Merciful;
> Far from the lips of the evil, such a kiss and embrace come
> to me. (D 581)

Another common poetic device is the juxtaposition of *dār* and *minbar,* "gallows and pulpit," by which poets from at least the days of Sana'i have symbolized the never-changing problem of the incompatibility of enraptured love and institutionalized religion. There are many hidden Mansurs who, relying upon the soul of Love, have dismissed the *minbars* and proceeded to the gallows, for all those who prefer immediate experience over law-bound behavior are persecuted by tradition-bound orthodoxy or, as modern interpreters would say, by the establishment. But for Maulana, the true lover is a gypsylike rope dancer, dancing on the gallows rope, and the day of death is a festive day for him.

Maulana loved Hallaj's story and therefore repeated time and again his call,

> Kill me, O my trustworthy friends,
> for in my being killed there is my life.

Rumi fitted those short Arabic lines into his Persian verses, where they appear again and again, and he also alludes to or even directly quotes other lines from Hallaj's poetical work. Hallaj, in whose life and work the superiority of love and suffering and the knowledge that death is the door to life was so central, rightly occupies an important place in Maulana's work, even though he is dwarfed by comparison with the overwhelming "beloved," Shamsuddin (who, incidentally, was very critical of both Hallaj and Bayezid, accusing them of making impious statements). Yet one often feels that Maulana regarded Hallaj in a certain way as his forerunner and could identify far more readily with him than with other historical mystics.

There is no dearth of descriptions of the ideal guide for the wayfarer, of the saint who has completely purified himself by walking on the narrow path of asceticism in preparation for the arrival of Love. He has annihilated himself in God and lost himself in Him to such an extent that he has become God's instrument, as the _hadīth an-nawāfil_ promises, that tradition, in which God speaks of those who are drawing nearer to Him by means of their own supererogatory acts, while He is hurrying to them even faster, until "I become his eye by which he sees, his ear by which he hears, his hands by which he grasps." The true saint is unaware of his own actions, like the Seven Sleepers (Sura 18/8–25), and as he has no control over his movements he may at times perform acts that look strange, even impious, to the outsiders. A typical example of this mysterious function of the saint is the Koranic story of Khidr's strange and apparently disastrous behavior (Sura 18/65–83), which seemed incomprehensible even to Moses, who, though a prophet, was not privy to the deepest secrets of the saints.

With one hand they quaff the pure wine of faith,
with the other hand they grasp the flag of *kufr,* infidelity.

(D 785)

Their power is such that "they can take the arrow back to the bow," and thus their prayers are heard.

But true saints are hidden: "My friends are under My domes," says the extra-Koranic Divine Word, and God alone knows them; they are covered and invisible, as though they were God's brides. They do not boast of their wondrous faculties, but on the contrary may hide under lowly, even despicable forms, as becomes clear from the tale of Kharaqani in the *Mathnawī.* This aspect of true saintliness is particularly evident from Maulana's deep loyalty to Salahuddin the goldsmith, whose spiritual wealth most people in Konya did not understand, let alone appreciate.

The presence of the saint is absolutely necessary for the disciple's guidance, for he takes the divine words into himself and utters them like a parrot behind the mirror, from whom the disciple is to learn to speak. Without such a guide, a journey of two days would take the seeker a hundred years, and "he who has no *shaykh,* his *shaykh* is Satan." Many are the dangers on the path, and only the man of God can show the devotee how to avoid the numerous pitfalls. Yet the saint lives in a world of his own. He is visited in the morning by spiritual beings, and age and time mean nothing to him; he is youthful and yet remembers the time before the creation of "the house of clay and water" (i.e., this universe), for he was together with God. Now he lives in God, walking in the midst of people, yet never separated from Him in whom he has annihilated his lowly qualities and with whose qualities he has qualified himself.

Maulana has described the ideal man of God in a poem that has been published and translated time and again. It shows him in full clarity, free from the four elements that constitute the created world, free from the needs of normal matter-bound people, dwelling in perfect serenity in the realm of Love eternal:

The man of God is drunken without wine,
The man of God is full without roast meat.

The man of God is all confused, distraught,
The man of God needs neither food nor sleep.

The man of God: a king in dervish's frock,
The man of God: a treasure in the dust.

The man of God is not of air nor earth,
The man of God: of water not, nor fire.

The man of God, he is a boundless sea,
The man of God rains pearls without a cloud.

The man of God has hundred moons and skies,
The man of God has hundred radiant suns.

The man of God knows through the Truth Divine,
The man of God is learned without books.

The man of God: no heresy, nor faith,
The man of God knows not of wrong or right.

The man of God rode from Not-Being, look!
The man of God comes here in glorious state.

The man of God is hidden, Shamsuddin!
The man of God: You seek and find him, heart!

8

The Chickpeas on the Spiritual Ladder

ONE OF THE MOST FASCINATING stories in Rumi's *Mathnawī* is that of the chickpeas (M II 4158ff.). The poet tells in ever so many words how the poor vegetables are being cooked and, complaining of the heat, try to jump out of the kettle. The housewife, however, explains to them that they must endure this trial for a little while, for having grown happily in the sunshine of God's kindness, they have now to experience also the fire of His wrath. Once they are thoroughly cooked and softened, they can be eaten by human beings and become part and parcel of human life, thereby to attain a higher rank on the ascending ladder of creatures. Here Maulana takes up an idea expressed long before him by Aristotle and Galen, that is, that food is cooked and refined in the body and finally transformed into semen so that it can indeed develop into a human being.

But there are other points to this seemingly quite funny kitchen story. One must never forget that for Rumi, as for his predecessors, "everything outside God is eating and being eaten"; the image of the cruel Frau Welt who devours her children comes to mind. Even more interesting is a note in Baha'-i Walad's *Ma'ārif* that must have been known to his son. Baha'-i writes:

I had eaten much. I saw in my stomach all the water and bread. God inspired me: "All this water, this bread, these fruits have tongues and praise Me with their voices and supplications. That

means human beings and animals and fairies are all forms of
nourishment that have turned into voices of supplication and praise
for Me. . . ." (p. 115)

Everything is eaten, and every food, whatever it may be, has a
tongue to remember the Lord. In light of these remarks, the
central role of food imagery in Maulana's work can be easily
understood.

The story of the chickpeas becomes important for various
reasons. First of all, it shows clearly Maulana's fascination with
food and kitchen imagery: besides remembering his father's strange
vision, he never ceases to remind his audience that everything that
is raw must be cooked, has to mature, or (in the case of cider) has
to ferment to become delicious wine. Humans are like kettles or
cauldrons, and from the smell that they exude one can deduce
their contents:

> You have drunk from the wine "Heedlessness" and have
> become a renegade:
> The stench of your mouth acknowledges that. (D 2261)

For this reason Maulana sometimes admonishes himself to put the
lid on the kettle "Speech" lest anyone understand his secrets and
recognize what is cooking. On the other hand, he frequently asks
his companion or his beloved: "What did you eat yesterday?" and
then wants to eat the same food, as if he could thus partake of the
friend's qualities by an act of spiritual or material communion.
However, the use of the word *dūsh,* "yesternight," in such questions
may also point to the primordial Yesterday, that is, the day of the
Covenant when God addressed the not-yet-created souls with the
word *Alast,* "Am I not your Lord?" For on that day before all days,
the drink of Love was distributed and each soul received its share
of the eternal spiritual food, a share according to which its life in

this world was to unfold. (Shamsuddin, so Rumi holds, was granted a particularly big sip from the wine of Love at that primordial banquet.) Kettles may be blackened by the heat and smoke of the kitchen, yet if they are made of gold, the external blackness cannot diminish their value. Such is the state of humans as well: if their essence is pure, the darkness and pollution of the material world cannot sully them.

Maulana sees kettles and kitchens everywhere:

> I want to draw a ladle full of blood from the kettle "Soul"
>
> (D 1691)

This is his state following the disappearance of the friend. But the soul is not only a kettle, it is also a kitchen, and so is the heart. Head and stomach are kitchens, each for a different kind of food, and "the Sufis remain hungry in the kitchen 'Intellect.' "

The wide use of kitchen-related imagery is all the more astonishing as Maulana himself was much given to fasting and devoted many poems to the "food of hunger"—that food which, according to traditional Sufism, is kept by God's side for His special friends. If one must eat, then it should be only a little and, more important, absolutely pure, ritually permitted food. For the Sufi should be so purified that even the foodstuff that comes from an uncertain source or the house of a sinner causes him to experience a disruption of his spiritual state, as Rumi indicates in a story in *Fīhi mā fīhi*, according to which a saint who unknowingly ate food taken from a woman's house had a nocturnal emission. Yet despite his own ascetic way of life, Maulana was thoroughly familiar with various dishes of Konya, and eggplant (which he apparently disliked) and sheep's feet (also not one of his favorites) appear in his verse along with *tutmaj*, a kind of vermicelli, and the usual poor man's food: whey and perhaps a bit of dried meat, *tharīd*. A shaving of turnip on a piece of bread looked to him like Satan's forelock.

We follow Maulana to the marketplace, where the druggist sells sugar in very small quantities, wrapping the precious commodity in little paper bags. We should not conclude, however, that his shop holds only such small quantities as these! In his stores are treasures of sugar, just as the treasures of heaven and earth are with God (Sura 15/21). But he gives according to the capacity of the recipient and dispenses his gifts and graces in smaller or larger measure. And if the sugar were to know how sweet are the beloved's lips, it would melt like water (D 1110).

Here in the marketplace, peaches imported from Laranda smile sweetly, just as the pomegranates laughingly show their teeth, that is, their shimmering red berries. In order to preserve vegetables and meat they had to be pickled, and Rumi may compare a sinister-looking individual to *turshū,* pickled vegetables. But he knows also, like his predecessors among the mystical poets, that salt can both preserve and purify: the comparison of the "spiritually transformed" human being to an ass who has fallen into a salt mine appears in Maulana's work as in Sana'i's poetry; the impure animal is completely transformed into the wholesome salt. Yet the comparison is far more poignant in the original than in translation, for salt in the Persian language is associated with loveliness: if one calls the beloved *bā-namak,* "salty," it means that he is lovely, "tasty," and delightful, and the elegant contrast of the friend's sugar lips with his "salt" is commonplace not only with Maulana. Besides, both sugar and salt were highly appreciated in the Middle Ages, as were all spices.

The most important part of Rumi's kitchen-related vocabulary deals with sweets. The Sufis had always been noted for their fondness for sweetmeats—probably a result of their long periods of fasting and their generally abstemious life, just as their occasional outbursts into crude, even obscene anecdotes was a reaction to the long periods of the hardest and most demanding ascetic discipline. Maulana himself was apparently fond of sweets, and the city of Konya was probably as famous for its sweets and varieties of halwa in those days as it is in our century—so much so that halwa and Konya are mentioned together in Turkish proverbs. We may well believe Rumi's story in *Fīhi mā fīhi* of the villager who had never enjoyed anything sweet but carrots, but when he came to town and was offered *halwa* he realized what he had been missing for years. The parable refers, of course, to the normal human being who enjoys mundane joys and suddenly realizes how much more wonderful are the spiritual joys, of which he has never before been aware. This theme, a favorite of Maulana's, is also elaborated—from a different vantage point—in the story of the Bedouin who brought brackish water as a gift to the caliph in Baghdad, for he was not aware of the endless amount of sweet water in the Tigris (M I 2708ff). As for the true dervishes, God Himself prepares the halwa for them (as Rumi sings in a lengthy poem featuring the recurring rhyme word *ḥalwā*), and the whole universe is, as it were, a huge pan in which the sweet is prepared, with the stars themselves serving as cooks.

Bread was the staple food in the Middle Ages, and for Rumi the development of the grain, which is crushed beneath the earth and awakens in spring to sprout into wheat or barley, is a fine image of life in general. For it is not enough that the grain must first suffer and be resurrected in the form of the ear: the stalks have then to be cut, the grains thrashed and ground in the mill, before the flour can be brought to the baker. There it must undergo yet another trial, that of entering the oven, before it can serve as nourishment for humans and thus, like the chickpeas, become part of human life (or, in other words, gain an opportunity to become spiritualized). Maulana loved this complex of images, which seemed to him most expressive of the constant suffering required for maturity. Only once does the description of the preparation of bread take an unexpected turn: in the *Mathnawī* lovemaking and dough-kneading are described in such lively and matter-of-fact images that one wonders whether they are to serve as metaphor for the apparently cruel but delightful ways in which Divine Love sometimes treats human beings, or whether, just for a moment, the sheer joy in sensual experience is being expressed without inhibition (M VI 3946ff.). In this passage one may detect the influence of Baha'-i Walad's very outspoken description of God's loving nearness.

But Maulana knows also that the wheat that will sprout from his own grave will be intoxicating. It is an old belief that the plants that grow on someone's grave reveal the state of the deceased person's heart: the suffering lover may sprout tulips, while on the tomb of one who still waits for his beloved to appear, the narcissus, symbol of the eye, will grow. Maulana therefore knows that everything that will grow from the soil of his dead body will be intoxicating and intoxicated—and rightly so. He clearly distinguished between the *bāda-i angūri,* the "grapewine" that is the share of the Christians, and the *bāda-i Manṣūrī,* the wine of Mansur Hallaj, which belongs to the lovers of God. Yet there is no dearth of wine poetry in his verse. For wine imagery was common to the Sufis, and it is highly probable that Maulana had read the great *Khamriyya,* the "wine ode" of his elder contemporary Ibn al-Farid in Egypt, for one of his long *ghazals* uses an imagery quite similar to that of the Egyptian master. "Intoxication" is the expression for that mystical state in which the human being no longer knows where or what he is, and the beginning of one playful *ghazal* has often been quoted:

> *Man mast u tū dīwāna—kay barad mārā khāna?*

> I drunk and you mad—who'll bring us back home?
> Did I not tell you: Drink two, three cups less?

Drunkenness is the state of highest spiritual happiness. Maulana therefore tells a story in the *Mathnawī* (M II 2392ff.) that has a modern ring to it: A police inspector, determined to check the breath of a man who seems unable to walk straight, tells the suspect to say "Ah!" But the Sufi says instead, "Hu, Hu!" (the dervish's cry "He! He!" at the close of the mystical exercises). The inspector finally becomes angry, but the stubborn suspect informs him that *Ah* is the expression of grief, while *Hu* is the expression of highest joy. Of course, he cannot persuade the policeman, who is utterly annoyed and finally tells him not to talk such silly Sufi nonsense but rather to get lost.

It is this kind of intoxication of which Rumi sings, the moment when the soul no longer sighs "Ah, ah!" but only thinks of the one, the Eternal He. The mystics' intoxication can reach such a stage that

> Yesterday we were intoxicated by the goblet,
>
> today the goblet is intoxicated by us. (D RUB. NO. 291)

Thus Maulana sings in a quatrain. For Divine intoxication is much higher than any effect of material wine upon the heart.

Wine can also serve as an image for man's development. There is the sour grape that is lovingly cooked by the sun's rays until it becomes sweet. On certain occasions the must that has been pressed out will be cooked for a long time until it reaches the stage of *pekmez,* a nourishing confiture of the consistency of honey, which in olden times was given to people, especially children, before they went out into the icy winter morning. Or the grapes may be treaded and left to ferment in the vat in order to become wine: in either case, the fate of the grape resembles that of the human soul, which has to undergo trials and tribulations to become mature and sweet.

There is yet another aspect to this development:

> No mirror turns to iron again;
>
> No wine turns to sour grapes again. (M II 1317)

The process is irreversible; the upward movement continues from stage to stage. This leads us to the second aspect of the story of the chickpeas.

Maulana, like his spiritual teacher Sana'i, was fond of the term "ladder," *nardibān*, which may imply an allusion to the Arabic term *mi'rāj*, "ladder." *Mi'rāj*, however, came also to denote the heavenly journey of the Prophet. Maulana sees ladders everywhere, from the *samā'*, the mystical dance that is the ladder that leads to the beloved's roof, to the education of mankind, which proceeds in slowly rising spirals. Within the creation, gourds and cucumbers are on the lowest rungs of the ladder of development, while humans have already reached a uniquely high position; yet each and every individual has to rise in his, her, or its own life, and human beings must undergo the hard discipline of the path to develop all their God-given talents and innate spiritual powers.

For this reason we find Maulana also as a teacher of the prescribed ritual duties as well as the supererogatory acts of the believer. Standing firmly on the revealed law of Islam, he teaches his listeners to perform the duties of the believers, the "five pillars of Islam": the profession of faith, the acknowledgment that "there is no deity save God," was the basis, and the mystics had directed their entire thought, love, and life to the one and unique God: how could someone with healthy eyes doubt the Unity of God? Only a poor squint-eyed individual may see two bottles instead of one and, through his insistence on there being two, smash the one existent bottle and be deprived of its precious contents (M II 3637 et al.). As for the second half of the profession of faith, "Muhammad is the Messenger of God," it was close to Maulana's heart and developed into a profound devotion to the leader of the community, the luminous Prophet (see pages 125ff.), whose light seemed to radiate through Shams.

The most important duty was ritual prayer, *ṣalāt*, Persian-Turkish *namāz*, for which Rumi developed an entire theology of his own (see chapter 9). The Koran always connects the duty of *ṣalāt* with that of *zakāt*, the alms tax that is to be paid in prescribed measure for a number of specified purposes in the community. This "pillar" does not much lend itself to poetic elaboration, but Maulana, like other Persian poets, sometimes alludes to the *zakāt-i la'l*, the tax to be paid on rubies. As the mouth of the beloved is often compared to a ruby, the *zakāt-i laʾl* means, in poetical parlance, a kiss that the lover wants to collect from his beloved.

However, the truly religious aspect of Maulana's verse is reflected in his numerous allusions to fasting, and a number of poems praise the fasting of the blessed month of Ramadan, when the Koran was first revealed and during which the pious can try to come closer to God with the help of the fast. For fasting means to come closer to the life of the angels:

> Gabriel's strength was not from the kitchen (M III 6f.)

as Rumi repeats, drawing upon various expressions known from early ascetics. Is it not so that those who eat straw become a sacrificial lamb, *qurbān,* while those who eat light are transformed into a Koran, *qur'ān?* (see D 729). Maulana therefore sometimes claims that the greatest of the five pillars is fasting, when one "drinks the wine of the spirit," and he sees fasting as the war machine, *manjānīk,* that destroys the fortress of darkness and infidelity. Fasting is also connected with Jesus, since his mother, Mary, had vowed a fast, and as she could not speak, her newborn son gave witness to her virginity and purity. As the place of Jesus is the fourth heaven, fasting may lead the faithful to that lofty range (D 2307). Fasting is always helpful, and thus, in Maulana's view, "the mother 'Fasting' comes kindly to her children" during the month of Ramadan (D 2375).

Yet despite this high regard for fasting as a purification ritual, Maulana knows that there is something higher, and that the drink of spirituality is not dangerous even when quaffed at daytime. (In the same way, he points out elsewhere, the union of souls does not require the ritual bath that is prescribed following bodily union.)

> I said to him: "It is the month of fasting, and daytime!" He
> said: "Quiet!

For the wine of the soul does not break the fast—don't be
afraid!" (D 1214)

The last of the five pillars, the pilgrimage to Mecca, does not
play as important a role in Maulana's work as one might expect. It
is said that the family visited Mecca during their journey from
Khorasan to Konya, but Maulana never mentions this actual
experience. On the contrary, in a few poems he expresses pity for
those who undergo the hardships of traveling and have to suffer
robbery at the hands of the Bedouins just because they want to
visit a house made of stone. He calls to his contemporaries:

> O you who've gone on pilgrimage—
>> where are you, where, oh where?
> Here, here is the Beloved!
>> Oh come now, come, oh come!
> Your friend, he is your neighbor,
>> he is next to your wall—
> You, erring in the desert—
>> what air of love is this?
> If you'd see the Beloved's
>> form without any form—
> You are the house, the master,
>> You are the Kaaba, you! . . .
> Where is a bunch of roses,
>> if you would be this garden?
> Where, one soul's pearly essence
>> when you're the Sea of God?
> That's true—and yet your troubles
>> may turn to treasures rich—
> How sad that you yourself veil
>> the treasure that is yours! (D 648)

The beloved is not bound to a house of stone in the desert but
lives in the heart of the believer, in the lover's soul, and

> The pilgrim kisses the black stone of the Kaaba
> because he thinks of the Beloved's lips. (D 617)

Maulana knew well the duties of every Muslim, he knew the *sharī'a,* the broad road of rules and regulations that everyone must follow, but he was also fully conversant with the steps of the narrow path, the *ṭarīqa,* which the ascetic and the Sufi must tread. Maulana had studied all this with Burhanuddin Muhaqqiq, but he never explains in detail the various aspects of the path or speaks at length of stations and stages, for he was very well aware that the actual progress of a soul is due to divine grace. The modern reader of works of Sufism who is confronted with many contradictory statements about this or that stage may realize, as Maulana did, that words can never fully explain the vast range of experiences and that probably a good number of scholarly-looking definitions were actually meant as *koans* to guide the disciple to a nonrational understanding of the truth behind a given stage.

However, like every other Sufi, Maulana teaches that the very beginning of the path is *tauba,* "repentance," which means that one has to turn away from the world and its pleasures toward the realms of spiritual values. Such repentance is necessary, and without it the whole path is closed, for if the first brick is not laid out correctly, the whole minaret will buckle and collapse.

A long story in the *Mathnawī* takes up the Koranic saying about repenting "a sincere repentance," *taubatan nāṣūḥan* (Sura 66/8). Here the adjective *nāṣūḥ* is interpreted as a personal name. Thus the story of Nasuh's repentance tells how a man manages to work as a servant in the ladies' bath without being discovered, but when the princess loses a precious jewel and a body search is conducted, Nasuh repents so intensely of his depraved way of life that by some miracle he is exempt from being searched, and he begins a new, spiritual life without returning to his former sinful occupation of massaging women in the bath (M V 2227ff.).

On the whole, however, repentance is, like all stages, something to be transcended:

> Asceticism has a broken wing, and repentance has
>   repented—
> How could the lovers have anything to do with repentance?

Thus Maulana asks in the *Dīwān* (D 2337), for, as he says elsewhere:

> Love is an affliction for repentance and punishes it—
> What has repentance to do with Love that devours
>   repentance? (D 1265)

One observes a typical phenomenon in Maulana's poetry: the ecstatic utterances in which the *Dīwān* abounds gradually give way to educational tales and ethical adages. For although Maulana does not discuss mystical stages and stations in a theoretical way, yet he may allude to them, especially to *tawakkul,* "trust in God," and *riḍā,* "contentment." In the case of *tawakkul,* he does not follow the absolute trust of the early ascetics, who would not even stretch out their hands to a dried melon rind, as they were not sure whether or not God had meant it for them; rather, he goes back to the word of the Prophet, who advised a Bedouin who asked him about *tawakkul:* "First tie your camel, and then trust in God!" Although God has arranged and planned everything, yet man has also the responsibility to do whatever he can to avoid misfortune and not to lead others into temptation.

Patience and gratitude, *ṣabr* and *shukr,* a traditional complementary pair of stages, appear comparatively frequently in Maulana's work: patience, of course, is "the key to joy," as stated in an Arabic proverb that Maulana quotes more than once, and the stories of the prophets in the Koran are elaborations of this truth. For God will rescue the patient one, just as He rescued Yusuf from the well and the prison and Jonah from the belly of the fish. Are not the flowers and trees in spring translators of the "fine patience" (Sura 12/18, 83) that they practiced in wintertime and for which they are now being recompensed? Growth is possible only with patience, for it takes many years for a tree to grow;

similarly, it takes many months until the sperm grows into a lovely human being, and another long period for the infant to develop into a being endowed with intelligence and faith. And how many centuries are required for a single perfected being, a prophet or a saint, to appear on earth! Maulana had learned this praise of patience from Sana'i, who elaborated these ideas in impressive verses. To show how stupid an impatient person is, Maulana invents a ludicrous story of a man who wanted to have a lion tattooed on his back, but, unable to bear patiently the pain of the tattooing needle, he decided first to have a lion without a tail, then without legs, then without a head, and finally without a body (M I 3002ff.). Yet much as Rumi admonishes his audience to practice patience, still he himself bursts out in confession:

My patience died the night that Love was born!

Rather, he even dares to claim:

No, that is wrong! For in His love
I am an unbeliever if I have even a little bit of patience!

(D 2908)

Maulana is more interested in the correlated attitude, that of gratitude, for:

Patience says always: "I bring the good tidings
of union from Him!"
But gratitude says always: "I'm the owner
of treasures vast from Him!"

(D 2142)

Gratitude is required in every moment; one has to thank God for the gift, then even for the denial of the gift, and finally for the very ability to thank. As Maulana well knows, gratitude is something "that shackles gifts" (as he mentions in a letter to Sultan 'Izzuddin as well as in *Fīhi mā fīhi*), for when someone feels that his gift is gratefully received he will lovingly give more. The relation of patience to gratitude is, as Maulana says with a pun, like that of aloe to sugar: *ṣabr* is *sabr*, *shukr* is *shakkar* (D 3010).

Man proceeds on the path in ever-alternating stages, which makes him understand that he is "between God's two fingers." Among these stages or stations are fear and hope, which have been described as the "two wings that bring the human soul to God." The farmer always hopes for a good harvest but fears that a hailstorm or a swarm of locusts may destroy the fields; likewise the heart always hopes for Divine Grace and yet fears that something may cause it to fall deep into the abyss of wrath. Maulana knows that

> The seaman is constantly on the planks of fear and hope
>
> (D 395)

but once the boat is shattered and the planks sink, he will be united with the Divine Ocean, where these states are no longer important. And yet, when it comes to evaluating fear and hope, Maulana is a strong advocate of hope, for to hope means to think well of God, and God—so the Sufis and in particular Rumi say—loves those who "think well of Him" and will deal with them the way they expect Him to act:

> Is there anyone who has sown the grain of hope,
> To whom the spring of God's grace has not given a
> hundredfold harvest? (D 1253)

There is, however, one station on the path that means more to Maulana than any other: *faqr*, "poverty." This is not the poverty of an ordinary beggar; rather, it is the state in which one knows that the creature is absolutely poor before the Creator, who is "the Rich, and you the poor," as the Koran states (Sura 35/15). *Faqr* is the quality of which the Prophet boasted when he said, "My poverty is my pride" (*faqrī fakhrī*), and it means to give oneself completely into God's hands. In this sense it is almost a coterminus with *fanā*, "annihilation," a state that leads one to lose everything in God's unfathomable wealth. "When *faqr* becomes complete, it is God"—this saying, known since the late twelfth century in the eastern Islamic world, appears once also in Rumi's verse. Maulana sees this *faqr* in his visions: it is like the *shaykh*, while everything else is like the circle of disciples around the master, or else it is "a mine of rubies" (D 2015), a reference to the most precious stone known to medieval gemology, radiant like the sun, which offers precious scarlet robes of honor to those who love it.   •

Thus Maulana leads his disciples on to higher and higher spheres until all stations and stages—not only those of repentance and patience—disappear and Love takes over. The Sufis have often tried to describe the final stage of Love or Intuitive Knowledge, gnosis, but they always found the task impossible, however many words they might invent. It is a state of *bīkhudī* ("selflessness"); *bīkhudī* is like the mysterious bird, the Huma, under whose wings everyone becomes a king (D 2775), and Maulana goes so far as to sing in a *ghazal* with the recurrent rhyme *bīkhudītar*, "I would like to be even more selfless" (D 1469). These ideas permeate his work, just as they can be found in the writings of hundreds of later Sufis. In his early poems, however—and only there—one finds one expression that seems very dangerous to a moderate Muslim's ear: the poet speaks of becoming *allāhī*, "deified" (D 599). The term is applied to Shams, who is asked:

> Are you the light of the Divine *(Allāhī)* Essence, or are you
> all *allāhī*?

One would have to translate *allāhī* as "one with God," with Allah, the revealed God of the Islamic tradition—a notion that is quite hard to accept. Yet in another verse Maulana uses *allāhī* as a simple term for "united with God," "annihilated in God":

> Every soul who has become deified, *allāhī*, enters the secret
> royal chamber—
> It was a snake and became a fish, it comes from the dust to
> the paradisiacal fountain *kauthar*. . . . (D 538)

The term *allāhī*, which shocks the reader who finds it for the first time in some of the most ecstatic verses, is, however, not Maulana's invention. His father had used it several times, as for him the goal of the seeker's path was to become *allāhī*, "deified."

Maulana was well aware that the goal of education was to produce a veritable *mard*, a "man of God," who then ultimately reaches the ocean of the Godhead. He tried to indicate several of the stages on this upward path, but he is also aware that the spiritual guide can help the soul only to a certain degree. The importance of the right guide, the right spiritual leader, is great, and many passages in both the *Mathnawī* and *Fīhi mā fīhi* warn the wayfarer not to fall into any of the numerous traps on the path. One can try to walk alone, but it is safer to travel in a caravan, provided that the company consists of kindred spirits. How many people have gone to India and Herat without looking for anything but trade, how many have found in Turkestan or China no goods other than ruse and hatred! Even more dangerous is it to follow false leaders. Such leaders resemble the blind who have fallen in filth and do not realize that the stench they exude will sicken even the houris of Paradise (M III 2095).

One may encounter even more dangerous companions while traveling. There are the greedy and there are the stupid, who are so intolerable that even Jesus, he who personified patience and love, fled before them into the wilderness because he could no longer stand them (M III 2595). But equally dangerous and annoying are the overintelligent, the hairsplitting philosophers, for, as Rumi states in a famous line:

> Love is from Adam, and cunning intellect from Satan!
>
> (M IV 1402)

The external sciences, when separated from their divine origin, are like a stable where animals may stay for a few days, that's all. What is more, one who interprets the Divine Word wrongly despite his scholarship is comparable to a fly, his imagination like an ass's urine, his conceptions like straw (M 11088). And Maulana complains—as every great mystic throughout the ages has done—that the scholars of his day know and understand all the external · problems (which are basically irrelevant) but do not know that which is closer to them than anything else, that is, their own soul, their individuality.

Let it be said, too, that Maulana also describes in quite colorful language other highly dangerous characters, namely the self-styled Sufis who shave their heads like gourds and whose talk is so pious and highfalutin that the gullible wayfarer considers them to be as great as Junayd or Bayezid, those models of classical Sufi thought (D 1093; cf M V 3807; M II 3508ff.).

So far we have dealt with two aspects of the story of the chickpeas: its importance for Rumi's metaphorical language, his kitchen-related vocabulary, and its importance as a paradigm for the twofold way of humankind: the broad way of the *sharī'a* and the narrow path of the Sufi *ṭarīqa,* which—it is hoped—will lead the seeker back to his eternal home. Yet there is still another aspect to the story. By being boiled and eaten, the vegetables will become part and parcel of the human beings who consume them and will be transformed into human qualities after they have contributed to the development of the semen; the semen, *manī,* in turn will develop into *manī,* "I-ness," "personality," as Rumi says in an elegant pun (D 863). This emphasis on everything's capacity to rise through the various levels of existence connects to a number of stories and deliberations, all of which are told in the third and fourth books of the *Mathnawī.* At the time when these books were written—the mid-1260s—Maulana seems to have been greatly interested in the problem of the ascending gamut of existence. His most famous expression of this problem is the following short poem:

> I died as mineral and became a plant,
> I died as plant and turned to animal.
> I died as animal and became man.
> What fear I, then, as I cannot diminish by dying?
> Once when I die as a human, I'll become an angel,
> and I shall give up angelhood,
> For Not-Being, 'adam, calls with an organlike voice:
> "Verily we are His, and to Him we return!" [Sura 2/151]
>
> (M III 3901)

Friedrich Rückert translated these lines into German more than one hundred and fifty years ago, but his poetical rendering omits the last line, which speaks of returning to 'adam, "Not-Being." Few poems in the Mathnawī have attracted as many commentators and interpreters, both Eastern and Western, as this one. The passage has usually been seen in connection with another poem, one, however, that is more diffuse and speaks of the world being a dream (M IV 3637ff.). It is also possible to find related remarks in a number of other, less outspoken passages and, rarely, in some late poems of the Dīwān.

Many interpreters have seen in the "I died as a mineral" the expression of the working of the one Divine Spirit through the various levels of existence; thus Reynold A. Nicholson, who saw it as a poetical rendering of a purely Neoplatonic idea. Others—in particular interpreters from twentieth-century India—found in it Darwinian evolutionism long before Darwin. Yet others saw the reflection of Aristotelian thought. In all these cases, however, the readers seem to have understood a somewhat mechanical principle at work—a principle of upward movement by which the lowliest creatures, beginning with parts of the mineral kingdom, are transformed in the course of aeons into something higher: the stone crumbles one day to become dust out of which plants grow; these in turn will be eaten by animals, and these again by human beings, who may in turn be able to reach the realm of pure spirituality.

This would be, I feel, too materialistic an explanation. Our chickpeas may help us better to understand the real meaning of the poem. "I died as a mineral" (M III 3901f.) for in the middle of their dialogue with the housewife (who represents the spiritual guide), the chickpeas are taught to sing:

> uqtulūnī yā thiqātī
>
> Kill me, O my trustworthy friends!

These are the words of the martyr-mystic al-Hallaj, who asked his contemporaries again and again to kill him so that the "I" that stood between him and his Divine Lord and Beloved might be annihilated. Maulana Rumi was clearly fond of Hallaj's verse, for he quotes it several times both in the *Dīwān* and in the *Mathnawī*, sometimes even expanding its wording. What Hallaj's verse means in our context is that the development to higher stages is no mechanical process but rather something that can be achieved, provided the creature willingly and lovingly sacrifices itself to a higher goal. It is reminiscent of the story of the moth that is drawn to cast itself into the flame in order to become part of the flame and to give up its ego voluntarily to attain to a higher life. This idea is perhaps most beautifully expressed in Goethe's famous poem "Selige Sehnsucht" ("Blessed Longing"), in which, drawing from Persian mystical texts, he sings of the mystery of the imperative *stirb und werde,* "Die and become," that is, "Die to this existence and be reborn on a higher level." Not in vain did the Sufis stress the injunction *Mūtū qabla an tamūtū,* "Die before you die," for every act of shedding off a lowly quality is a small death; every sacrifice for the sake of others is another small death whereby the individual gains new spiritual value; thus, in a series of deaths, the soul rises to immortality or to a level of spiritualization that it has never dreamed of. This idea, I believe, underlies Rumi's story of the chickpeas: he wants to teach his listeners and readers that only by constant sacrifice is development possible. It is pain, willing acceptance of pain, that helps in this process:

> What does the ascetic seek? Your compassion [raḥmat].
> What does the lover seek? Your pain [zaḥmat].
> That one dead in the cloak,
> this one alive in the shroud! (D 1804)

To be sure, each of the interpretations offered by scholars has its value, and they are probably all true to some extent. Maulana's words are often ambiguous, and one has to listen carefully to the overtones—and in this case, the quotation from Hallaj seems to offer at least one key for our understanding. For through the imagery complex of kitchen and cooking, the shedding off of old forms and the reaching of higher levels are intended, and Maulana has called his audience in so many ways to die in love in order to be resurrected. One can even say that the whole of the *Dīwān* revolves around this central idea. The chickpeas are part of his worldview, according to which the most important duty of every created being is to move on to the next higher level. Life is a constant journey, a journey that entails separation for the sake of union:

> Oh, if a tree could wander
> and move with foot and wings!
> It would not suffer the ax blows
> nor feel the pain of saws!
> For if the sun did not wander
> away in every night—
> How could at ev'ry morning
> the world be lighted up?

And if the ocean's water
    did not rise to the sky,
How would the plants be quickened
    by streams and gentle rain?
The drop that left its homeland,
    the sea, and then returned—
It found an oyster waiting
    and grew into a pearl.
Did Yusuf not leave his father,
    in grief and tears and despair?
Did he not, by such a journey,
    gain kingdom and fortune wide?
Did not the Prophet travel
    to far Medina, friend?
And there he found a new kingdom
    and ruled a hundred lands.
You lack a foot to travel?
    Then journey into yourself,
And like a mine of rubies
    receive the sunbeams' print!
Out of yourself—such a journey
    will lead you to your self,
It leads to transformation
    of dust into pure gold!
Leave bitterness and acid,
    go forth to sweetness now!
For even brine produces
    a thousand kinds of fruits.
It is the Sun of Tabriz
    that does such wondrous work,
For every tree gains beauty

when touchèd by the sun.

Yusuf—so the poet explains in this poem—was forced to leave his father and undergo imprisonment in order to emerge, finally, as the "mighty one in Egypt"; the Prophet himself had to leave his hometown and migrate to Medina to become the ruler there. Is not every drop that comes from the ocean on its way back home, in the hope of becoming a pearl? No drop could dream of being transformed into a pearl unless it had taken upon itself the hardships of the journey. Why, then, should we not participate in this upward movement?

It is the journey toward the primordial home, the journey on which Mustafa the Prophet is the caravan leader. It will lead the human soul to the radiant summits of *kibriyā,* Divine Glory, and finally to *'adam,* the unfathomable abyss of the Divine Essence.

Sultan Walad tells about his father's teacher, Burhanuddin, that he was asked:

> "Has the road an end or not?" He answered: "The road has an end, but the stations have no end, for the journey is twofold, one to God and one in God." (VN 237)

'Attar before him, at the end of his *Mantiq ut-tayr,* had given the same explanation of the infinite journey.

Many mystics, especially those in the centuries after Rumi, have classified this journey to "the City of God at the other end of the road" in exact stations, or in forty steps, and have given rules and regulations for the travelers. Maulana does not bother about such details. He knows that once the heart is set upon its journey it will go, no matter what the speed, and it may be grasped unawares by the falcon "Love," to be carried into a presence that is higher than reason. It is out of this conviction that Maulana writes lines that refute Omar Khayyam's skepticism and teach us, as the housewife taught the pot-herbs, that Love is the moving spirit and the goal of life:

One handful of dust says: "I was a tress!"
One handful of dust says: "I am a bone!"
You will be confused—then Love suddenly comes:
"Come closer! I am Life eternal for you!" (D 1515)

9

Prayer: The Divine Gift

MAULANA'S BIOGRAPHER SIPAHSALAR tells how the master spent
one night in prayer in the mosque. It was the dead of winter, and
in the course of praying he wept so profusely that his beard, wet
by his tears, froze and clung to the ground. Thus his disciples had
to rescue him in the morning. This story may sound exaggerated,
even absurd to a modern reader, yet, it well conveys the intensity
of Maulana's devotional life. Perhaps it was during that night that
he sang one of his most moving *ghazals,* whose lively swinging
rhythm reflects the fast beating of his heart:

> At the time of evening prayer
>> everyone spreads cloth and candles,
> But I dream of my beloved,
>> see, lamenting, grieved, his phantom.
> My ablution is with weeping,
>> thus my prayer will be fiery,
> And I burn the mosque's doorway
>> when my call to prayer strikes it. . . .
> Is the prayer of the drunken,
>> tell me, is this prayer valid?
> For he does not know the timing
>> and is not aware of places.
> Did I pray for two full cycles?

Or is this perhaps the eighth one?

And which Sura did I utter?

For I have no tongue to speak it.

At God's door—how could I knock now,

For I have no hand or heart now?

You have carried heart and hand, God!

Grant me safety, God, forgive me. . . . (D 2831)

He feels like the shadow that moves only when the sun moves; he has no will of his own, does not know what he does, cannot count the cycles of prostrations and movements in prayer. He is carried away by the passion of his love. Is such a prayer licit at all? For the Koran says, "Don't approach prayer when you are drunk" (Sura 4/ 46), and his intoxication is surely deeper than any drunkenness induced by worldly wine.

Maulana once described himself as completely transformed into prayer, "so that everyone who sees me wants a prayer from me." Thus it is understandable that in a number of lyrical poems the borderline between love poem and prayer is blurred, or that the poet easily switches from what first seems to be an ecstatic love verse to a deep-felt prayer, from an expression of yearning for Shams to lines that seek help from God or praise Him in ever-new words.

Thus prayer is one of the most important features in Maulana's work. There are scenes in the *Mathnawī* wherein he describes the various aspects of ritual prayer, beginning with the necessary preparation—that is, the ablutions; here he jokes about a silly man who recited all the prescribed formulas to be uttered while purifying the limbs and parts of the body, but in the wrong sequence: thus, when performing abstersion he would say, "O God, grant us the scent of Paradise!" instead of the correct "O God, cleanse us from defilement," and so on. Such a person, Maulana holds, is the perfect example of the well-meaning but stupid individual who never understands the true meaning of what he says and simply parrots empty words and gestures (M IV 2213).

Maulana knows, too, that each of us turns in our prayers—that is, in our thoughts and wishes—to a different *qibla,* "prayer direction," and each person has a different *qibla.* Late in his life he enumerates the various directions that people's longing thoughts take:

> The Kaaba for the spirits
> > and Gabriel: the Sidra-tree,
> The *qibla* of the glutton:
> > that is the tablecloth.
> The *qibla* for the gnostic:
> > the light of union with God.
> The *qibla* of philosophy,
> > of reason, is: vain thought!
> The *qibla* of the ascetic:
> > the beneficent God.
> The *qibla* of the greedy:
> > a purse that's filled with gold.
> The *qibla* of those who look at
> > true meaning, is patience fine.
> The *qibla* of those who worship
> > just forms: an image of stone.
> The *qibla* of those esoterics
> > is He, the Lord of Grace.
> The *qibla* of these exoterists
> > is but a woman's face. . . . (M VI 1896)

This graphic description of the various directions of prayer, symbolizing the goals of human beings, was so well known among Persian-speaking Muslims that it was considered in India "a kind of commentary on the Koran," as Mrs. Meer Hasan Ali, an

Englishwoman who lived in Lucknow in the early nineteenth century, learned from her Muslim friends.

Maulana knew all the approaches to prayer. One of his most impressive descriptions of ritual prayer is found in the story of how Daquqi led the prayer along with his shipwrecked companions: they were like satin, and he like the precious *tirāz* embroidery, and when he uttered the words *Allāhu akbar,* "God is greater [than everything]" they became, as it were, "sacrificial lambs" before God, for the words *Allāhu akbar* are also said when slaughtering an animal for sacrifice (M III 334off.). Thus Maulana makes his audience feel that to enter into ritual prayer means to give oneself completely and unconditionally to God: one leaves the world of matter behind and senses oneself in the presence of the highest Lord. This sense of awe, often mentioned by the pious and even more by the mystical writers of Islam, is the feeling that Adam expresses in his great prayer when contemplating God's majesty and grace: whatever He does, is correct:

> If You don't grant the way,
>> know that the soul is lost:
> The soul that without You
>> lives on—take it as dead!
> If you ill-treat Your slaves,
>> if You reproach them, Lord,
> You are the King—it does
>> not matter what You do,
> And if You say the sun,
>> the lovely moon are "filth,"
> And if you say that "crooked"
>> is yonder cypress slim,
> And if You say the Throne
>> and all the spheres are "low,"
> And if You call the sea

and gold mines "needy, poor"—
>
> That is permissible,
>
> for You're the Perfect One:
>
> You are the One who can
>
> perfect the transient! (M 1 3899ff.)

Such prayer poems reflect Maulana's own attitude, his ceaseless amazement in the presence of the Mighty Lord. He knows the power of a prayer that comes from a pure heart, and he chastises those who call upon God only in time of danger and afterward forget Him: here the poet takes up once more the argumentation of the Koran, which often warns and reproaches these people, yet even when one has forgotten God for a long time one can return to Him; it is never too late for repentance. The story of the old harpist (M 1 2083f.) exemplifies this. A musician had enjoyed life for many long years, but finally his voice had become "like the voice of the ass" (which according to Sura 31/18 is "the most unpleasant voice") and his harp was out of tune, many of its strings torn.

> He spoke: "You gave me life,
>
> and gave me ample time,
>
> You were so kind to one
>
> who is so lowly, God!
>
> For seventy full years
>
> I was rebellious here—
>
> But You did not withhold
>
> Your bounty for one day!
>
> Today, I cannot earn;
>
> I'm old, I am Your guest,
>
> I'll play the harp for You,
>
> for I belong to You!"

And the Lord does not disappoint the sinner who comes and takes refuge in His boundless Mercy.

If the old sinner's prayer is accepted, so too will other prayers, especially those offered for others, always be heard and accepted. Maulana goes even further: he describes the amazement of the audience when a preacher prayed not only for his friends and his family but also for his enemies and for those who had treated him badly, for highway robbers and other criminals. Asked the reason for seemingly so strange a prayer, he explained that these evil people had mistreated him so badly that they had forced him to seek the help of God and so had inadvertently turned him back to the path of virtue and brought him closer to his Lord; hence they deserved his gratitude, for they were his helpers on the way to God (M IV 56).

God hears the prayer of each and every one, though it may not be uttered in a style that appears correct to theologians or to the clergy. He will not spurn the sigh of a menstruating woman, even though in her impurity she is not supposed to perform the ritual prayer or recite the Koran. Maulana's most famous story in this connection is that of the shepherd's prayer, in which Moses, the stern lawgiver-prophet, is horrified by a simple shepherd's words:

> Moses saw a shephered on the road,
> Saying: "You who choose the one You want:
> Where are You, that I become Your servant,
> That I mend Your frock and comb Your hair,
> That I wash Your garment, kill Your lice,
> Bring You milk, O Highest of the High!
> Kiss Your darling hand, massage Your feet well,
> That I sweep Your little room at bedtime!
> Sacrificed be all my goats to You
> Whom I think of, yearning, full of love!" (M II 1720ff.)

Moses, confused, asks the shepherd whom he addresses, and when the poor man replies that he is talking to God, Moses tells him to stuff cotton in his mouth and be gone. But then God reveals to

His stern messenger that He has sent him not to separate people but to unite them. The prophet is to respect everyone's ways of worship, for He, the Lord, understands the stammering child as a mother would understand it, and in fact, these simple words that come from the heart are to be preferred over the sophisticated formulas that a prophet or priest may devise. Finally, everyone has the right to address the Lord in his own language, for

> The Sindhis like the expression of Sind,
> The Hindis like the expression of Hind,

and God knows all languages and understands the silent sigh that comes from a lover's heart. On hearing the Lord's harsh words, Moses repents and runs into the desert to seek the shepherd and to apologize for his words, but when he finally finds him, the shepherd has left the stage of childish speech and has reached a higher life of union with the One to whom he had prayed. Such stories led Maulana also to insert remarks into his verse that may sound absurd to proper theologians and even more so to skeptical intellectuals. Although Maulana felt that every prayer reaches God, yet there is no doubt that not every prayer is answered, nor every wish fulfilled. It is a problem with which theologians of all religions have wrestled. And more: is it meaningful, indeed, even permissible to pray, since God has predestined everything from the day of creation? Certain Sufis saw no need for prayer but rather taught silent acceptance of whatever was "written" for them, yet most of them relied on God's promise in the Koran: "Call Me, and I shall answer!" (Sura 40/62)—this Divine Word, Ghazzali held, is proof of man's high rank in creation. Maulana follows him in this respect: the dialogue between man and God is the most precious part of life. Prayer and affliction work together, for prayer is like a shield that protects man from the arrows of affliction—and it is not prohibited to carry a shield in battle!

Why, then, is not every prayer answered? Or why does it often take so long for a positive answer to come? Maulana's explanation relies upon an alleged *ḥadīth* which is found and elaborated in the *Risāla,* the "Treatise on Sufism" by the eleventh-century Sufi al-Qushayri. Human beings are comparable to birds: does one not put nightingales and parrots in cages to enjoy their sweet voices? Just as we like to listen to the voices of caged birds, so God, too, enjoys the voices of human beings: He keeps them for some time in a difficult position so that they will continue to call on Him and pray to Him with their sweet, sad voices. Or else, as Rumi continues, when an old, ugly beggar asks for a piece of bread, one immediately gives him something so that he may disappear as quickly as possible; but if a young, handsome person begs for bread, one keeps the supplicant waiting under one or another pretext in order to look at the lovely face a little longer. God, too, loves to look at His friends and therefore tests them that they may supplicate Him again and again (M VI 4227ff.).

This sounds like an all too anthropomorphic explanation of the mystery of prayer, yet even under the childish surface it reveals Maulana's deep trust in Divine Wisdom. Besides, he knew very well and frequently remarks that not every prayer can be answered, as the wishes of humans are conflicting and often absolutely contrary. God, however, knows best what is good for humankind and for the great plan according to which He has created and maintains the universe. One therefore owes Him thanks for not answering a prayer, for one should understand that the fulfillment of this or that wish would have ultimately led to destruction. Transformation of the mind is the meaning of prayer, and the seeker who fully trusts in God's eternal Wisdom will recognize a sign of grace even in the rejected prayer and will thank God for not answering his request (M II 139ff.).

Prayer, as the Koran states, is a prerogative of humans, who may call to God. But Maulana knows—again from the Koran—that the world was created in order to worship God and that everything praises the Creator in its own mute eloquence. He sees the flowers in spring engaged in prayer; the lily stands upright and calls out "*Allāhu akbar*"; the violet bows over its green prayer rug (D 805), and the trees lift their hands as though they were imploring God's help. They sing His praise without tongues when He grants them green robes in spring, and they ask for His support when their branches bend under their heavy load of fruit in the fall (D 2046). Birds too have their own songs of praise; and those who have ears to hear understand the hymns of all created beings and try to join in their laud. But there are times when one seems lost in absolute solitude; when no answer comes day after day, month after month, and one despairs and asks, "Is there any God at all?" This is the theme of the first story to be translated into a Western language from the *Mathnawī*. It appeared in Latin in 1821, in a booklet by the young German Protestant theologian F. D. A. Tholuck, called *Ssufismus sive theosophia persarum pantheistica*. It is an anthology culled from Persian and Turkish manuscripts in which the author—as is evident from the book's title—tries to show the "pantheistic" aspect of Sufism. The story selected from Rumi tells of a man who prayed for a long time without hearing any answer. At last Satan prevailed over him, so that he gave up prayer. But then he heard the Divine Voice:

> Your call "O God!" is My call "I am here."
> Your supplication is My message, dear,
> And all your striving to come close to Me
> Is but a sign that *I* draw you to Me.
> Your loving quest and pain: signs of My grace!
> In each "O God!" a hundred "Here's My Face!" (M IV 189ff.)

Tholuck himself found this story absurd and, good Protestant theologian that he was, feared it might lead to self-deification. But many decades later the Swedish historian of religion and archbishop Nathan Söderblom published the story in one of his works, *Främmande Religionsurkunder*, and since the beginning of the twentieth century it has been the most popular tale quoted in the West from Maulana's work, as it shows that Islam, too, has the concept of the *oratio infusa,* the prayer of grace. It should, however, not be taken as the sole instance of this theme in Maulana's work; on the contrary, many verses in the *Mathnawī* emphasize the fact that "He lights the candle of prayer in darkness." As all activity comes from God and begins with Him, and as His address precedes every human word, thus it is He who teaches man to pray:

> Otherwise, how could a rose grow out of an ash pit?
>
> (M II 2443ff.)

How could a poor human being dare address the mighty Lord? How would the heart dare call to the Eternal Beloved? Yet it is He who hears the unspoken prayer, and seen from this angle, every prayer is, in itself, its own answer. By praying, one acknowledges God's greatness and at the same time offers gratitude toward Him who not only has granted life and material goods but, what is more important, has granted a heart that can seek and find Him. He would never inspire someone to pray unless He would listen to him.

Prayer is the highest way to communicate with God. A word ascribed to the Prophet states that ritual prayer is *mi'rāj,* "ladder," and, more specifically, "heavenly journey." Rumi takes up this saying: the Prophet experienced God's immediate Presence in his nightly journey and could talk with Him without veils (while Gabriel had to remain behind), and he alluded to this moment with the words *lī ma'a Allāh waqt,* "I have a time with God." So too the heart of one who prays "has a time with God" when nothing stands between that heart and God. Once, when Mu'inuddin Parwana asked Maulana whether there was another way to God, higher than ritual prayer, Maulana replied that ritual prayer is a body; it is the outward form because it has a beginning and an end, for "everything that is expressed in sounds and words and has a beginning and an end, is a form and a body. . . ." And he continues:

Besides, the prophets have invented ritual prayer. As for our Prophet, who has clearly shown this rite of prayer, he said: "I have a time with God in which neither a God-sent prophet nor an angel who is brought near to God has room. Thus we learn that the soul of the ritual prayer is not alone this form. It is, rather, absorption and loss of consciousness, wherein all these outward forms remain outside and no longer have any room. Even Gabriel, who is a spiritual being, does not fit into it.

Maulana exemplifies this lesson with a story of his father, who had completely lost consciousness in prayer and had become himself "the light of God," so that those of his disciples who prayed facing him were preferred by God over those who prayed toward the actual prayer direction. When the person who prays has immersed himself in the Divine Presence, this world no longer exists for him; there is only bliss unspeakable, and silence, prayer without words:

> Become silent and go by way of silence toward
>   nonexistence,
> And when you become nonexistent, you will be all praise
>   and laud! (D 2628)

10

The Manifestations of Love

"What is the lover's state?" Thus asked a man.
I said to him, "Don't ask such questions, dear:
When you become like me, you'll know for sure;
The moment when He calls you, you will call! (D 2733)

HOW CAN LOVE BE EXPLAINED? The intellect attempting to convey it is like an ass in the morass, and the pen that is to describe it breaks into pieces. Thus says Maulana in the very beginning of the *Mathnawī*, in the initiatory scene in which young Husamuddin asks the poet about his relation to Shams, the Sun, compared with which the "sun in the fourth heaven is but an atom." He knows that he can never speak of it correctly, and yet his whole work is an attempt to explain this Love which removed him from his normal life and transformed him into a poet whose words are but a never-ending commentary on this Divine Mystery.

As the human heart is the "astrolabe of Love," showing its various aspects and positions, Maulana tries to describe or rather to circumscribe this power in ever-new images, in weird paradoxes, in touching little dialogues between his heart and the overpowering force. Rarely, in fact, does he repeat himself. There are poems that seem one long, jubilant song born of happiness in the beloved's presence; there are tender little lullabies for the soul who happily slumbers under the shadow of the friend's tresses, and other lines whose cruel images and cries of despair make the listener shiver. Images follow one upon another in breathtaking speed but with no apparent logical order: Love is pre-eternal, it is a magnet; for a moment it completely annihilates the soul, then again it is a trap to ensnare the soul-bird to which it offers a sip of the wine of Reality, and all this "is only the beginning of Love—nobody reaches its end!" Maulana likes to converse with Love to find out what it looks like:

> One night I asked Love: "Tell me truly, who are you?
> It said: "I am life eternal, I multiply the lovely life."
> I said: "O you who are beyond each place, where is your
> home?"
> It said: "I am together with the heart's fire and beside the
> wet eye,
> I am a dyer; due to me every cheek turns saffron-colored.
> I am a swift-footed messenger, and the lover my lean steed.
> I am the crimson of the tulip, the merchandise's worth,
> I am the sweetness of lament, the unveiler of all that is
> veiled. . . ." (D 1402)

One of the great odes in which Maulana tries to discover what Love is begins with the question

> O Love, who is more harmoniously shaped, you, or your
> garden and apple orchard? (D 2138)

And the poem continues in dancing rhythms to tell of the miraculous acts of Love, inspiring every atom, inducing the trees into dance, transforming everything:

> Through Love all that is bitter will be sweet,
> Through Love all that is copper will be gold.
> Through Love all dregs will turn to purest wine;
> Through Love all pain will turn to medicine.

Through Love the dead will all become alive,

Through Love the king does turn into a slave! (M II 1529f.)

Without Love there would be no joy in life, for "life would have no taste without its boundless salt." Its vision calls the wanderer home:

I traveled onward, I went from end to beginning:

This elephant saw in his dream the vast desert of your

Hindustan!

Hindustan stands here, as so often in medieval Persian literature, for the eternal home that the soul suddenly recalls in a happy dream. Then it longs to tear off the fetters that keep it here in the western exile of matter and run home, in an intoxicated dance, to rejoin the primordial jungle from which it was once captured. The elephant that dreams of India is like the nightingale who longs for the rose garden, like the reed flute that sings of the primordial reed-bed.

Rumi knows, and at the end of a long poem devoted to the aspects of Love even says, that one cannot speak enough of Love's face (or "faces") to the very day of resurrection, for

How can your ocean be measured with a saucer?

In other verses Love appears as the mirror for both worlds, or else as the power that polishes steel to transform it into a mirror. The opaque density of matter can become lucid thanks to its work, which is thus as essential as it is painful.

But Love appears also as a *muṣḥaf,* a copy of the Koran that the lover reads in his dreams, or it is the tablet from which he copies his poetry; this latter image is a fitting expression for the mystery of inspiration, for Maulana often did not know intellectually what he was singing. Similar is the idea that Love holds the poet in its fingers like a pen, so that he writes without being aware of the contents. But he knows: Shamsuddin's name was written in the notebooks of Love from the days of the Primordial Covenant.

Maulana uses Arabic and Persian, sometimes also drawing on Turkish and Greek expressions to speak of his feelings, and yet he knows that Love's beauty cannot be contained in all vessels, "even if I should praise it in a hundred thousand tongues." For it is, like God, both manifest and hidden. The lover can "travel in Love" and find greater happiness the farther he progresses, for Love is infinite, being divine, and it is greater than a thousand resurrections: resurrection is a limit, but Love is limitless.

As mystics and philosophers have ever held, Love is the reason for every movement in the world, for

> If the earth and mountains were not lovers,
> Grass could never sprout out of their breasts. . . . (D 2674)

Just as it sets everything in motion, so it also attracts everything: it is like amber, the "straw robber," *kahrubā,* but it attracts not only tiny wisps of straw (which resemble the lover's pale cheeks) but even the mighty mountains (a pun on the words *kāh,* "straw," and *kūh,* "mountain"). It is a magnet, drawing to it all hearts, these tiny iron slivers. Such ideas were commonplace in the writings of Persian thinkers and poets at that time (and are seen, for instance, in Avicenna's "Treatise on Love," but also in Nizami's poetical "Quintet"); Maulana, however, on the whole prefers images in which the living power of Love, not a mere mechanical attraction, becomes clear, and his tendency to use images drawn from everyday life shows itself in this sphere particularly well. Love is thus a school. Mystics have often referred to the educational value of human "metaphorical" love as a preparation for divine "real" love; but in Rumi's school, where God Most High is the teacher, worldly scholarship is sheer ignorance, for this school is made of fire. Love seizes the devotee's ear each morning to drag him off to school whether he wants it or not, and even the villagers (who in Maulana's work generally represent the base instincts and unbridled passions) are taught in the school of Love to read from the tablet of the invisible world.

Rumi once heard Love tell him that he himself was fire, kindled by Love's wind, but his favorite imagery describes the situation in reverse:

> Love is a fire that would turn me to water, if I were a hard
> stone. (D 2785)

The living flame of Love inspires him, and like the sun this flame can burn away everything, including thousands of material suns. Yet Maulana enjoys the fire—for his soul is a salamander and cannot live outside the fire. Just as in the Koranic story of Ibrahim (Sura 21/69), this fire becomes "cool and pleasant" to the lover, as if he were residing in a rose garden. What is more, it immolates every image, every form, and thus annihilates human faults and defects, so that no thorns remain and everything is turned into rose beds.

In one beautiful image Rumi compares Love to lightning whose flash burns the cloud that hides the moon: whatever may still veil the moonlike countenance of the beloved is destroyed.

The image of hearts and livers being roasted in the fire of Love is common among Persian and Turkish poets, and so is the scent of burning livers that ascends to the beloved's house as though it were a burnt offering. Does not Love turn man into an 'īd, a "feast" (presumably a reference to the Feast of Offerings during the pilgrimage to Mecca) and burn him like 'ūd, the precious aloeswood whose fragrance was used to perfume the imperial palaces? Or the lover may be likened to sipand, the seeds of wild rue that were burned in order to avert the evil eye from the friend's beauty. Love is a tannūr, an oven, to warm those frozen in the hibernal world of matter, and it is also the fire beneath the crucible in which the base metal melts, awaiting its transformation by Love's alchemy into pure, unalloyed gold. For Love requires that everyone who seeks it must enter the crucible (D 601)—a traditional image, but one that gains special charm when it occurs in a poem that bears the name of Salahuddin the goldsmith as a pseudonym for Maulana himself.

Images related to the realm of fire are always connected with suffering, even if this suffering is necessary and hence joyful. But the Sufis had invented a fine pun: when, at the time of the Primordial Covenant, the not-yet-created humanity responded to God's question *A-lastu bi-rabbikum,* "Am I not your Lord?" with the word *bala,* "Yes, certainly" (Sura 7/172), people accepted all the affliction, *balā,* that was to visit them in His service, and that means for the mystics, in the path of Love:

> Before people it is called Love;
> but before me it is the affliction, *balā,* of the soul! (D 2499)

Grief and worry are necessary in love, yet they have no real value:

> Only the eunuch "Grief" may enter the secret chamber of
> Love,

says Rumi in a daring image (D 1405).

To return once more to the fiery sphere: in Maulana's version of the moth that immolates itself in the candle, the flame appears to the fluttering creature (a classic image of the soul!) as a window, a window that opens onto the infinitude of Love's fiery ocean. But he also speaks of the "lamp of Love," and in an ecstatic, dancing poem he invites the lovers to allow their nutlike bodies and brains to be thrashed and beaten so that they may become oil in Love's lamp (D 2560). Even more grotesque is his comparison of the lover to an ostrich, a bird who, according to ancient and Oriental belief, swallows live coals. In an ecstatic *ghazal* with the opening lines

> When Love comes: "Do you hand your soul to me?"
> Why don't you say at once: "I will, I will!"

Maulana has the following vision:

Love like a tower of light,

Inside the tower of light: what a fire!

Like ostriches, the souls around that tower:

Their food, a most delicious fire! (D 2690)

In this fiery sphere the sun, always associated with Shams of Tabriz, is the most comprehensive and most covenient symbol of Love. At times, Rumi's descriptions of Love, his hymns to this Sun of Love, reach cosmic heights.

But if Love is fire, it is also water. It is the *kauthar,* the paradisiacal fountain—for it is "a fire that shames the Water of Life." Or:

Love is an ocean with invisible waves:

The ocean's water is fire, and its billows are pearls. (D 1096)

As Love is God's inmost essence, it appears as an ocean without end, even though its waves are blood or fire. The lover is either drowned there or swims around like a happy fish; no matter how much the fish may drink, the ocean never diminishes, for it is the beginning and end of everything.

But Love can appear also as a powerful torrent that washes away everything, and if Love can provide a purification by fire, so can it offer a purification by water. In fact, Love longs for those who are dirty, that it may wash away their impurities. Here again, Rumi becomes very specific:

There is no veil for the soul in the hot bath of his love;

I am no painting on the bathhouse wall—why should I not

rend my clothes [in loving ecstasy]? (D 1433)

The words "painting on the bathhouse wall" mean something lifeless, something that cannot be moved by the healthy hot water in which the living body submerses itself.

As Love is the ocean, so too it is rain. For when the clouds of

Love come, the dead earth will be fertilized (an image often used in connection with the Prophet of Islam):

> How happy the meadow where roses and eglantines are
>   grown
> From the water of love, and where yonder gazelles are
>   grazing! (D 2392)

Therefore, grass and leaves, symbol of humankind, should happily endure the rain, although it may whip them soundly for a time.

The positive, wholesome aspects of Love can be expressed more readily in the realm of water than in that of fire, for comparisons drawing on water imagery offer themselves without difficulty: Love is the veritable Water of Life that is hidden in the darkness, but Love can also be Noah's ark, or a boat that moves along softly while the lover slumbers peacefully. Love not only is water but also brings water:

> When the water carrier "Love" shouts with the voice of
>   thunder,
> The desert will soon be filled with greenery! (D 1308)

And here we are led to the imagery of spring, for Love comes like spring into the garden of the soul. Even more: Love itself is a garden, a garden that knows neither spring nor fall. It is watered by the sea of the eyes; that is, it blossoms when the lovers shed tears of longing, and its every thorn is more glorious than all the roses of our world. Hence Maulana, prefiguring scores of later Persian, Turkish, and Urdu poets, can claim that Love "keeps rose gardens in the midst of veils of blood." One has to read Rumi's spring poems in this light—it is Love's garden, where the trees perform the mystical dance and the birds sing of the beloved's beauty.

Love can also be seen as a tree, while the lovers are its shade and move with its branches as they swing. But this tree of Love can be described only in paradoxes: its branches are in preeternity, its roots in eternity, and it has no beginning or end in the world of time and space. Rumi invents comparisons that may at first appear absurd, yet make perfect sense: Love is like a creeping plant that completely surrounds the tree (natural man), suffocating it down to the last twig so that in the end only Love remains.

There are many other ways to speak of Love. It can be a kingdom, a town, a vast metropolis; it may the "Damascus of Love," recalling the city where Maulana rediscovered his lost friend Shams, or Egypt, the place where Yusuf, the paragon of beauty, dwells and whence caravans with sugar arrive. Perhaps there is a secret Baghdad where Love, the caliph, resides—for at the time these verses were written, Baghdad was still the seat of the Abbasid caliph.

Whether Love is a strong fortress or a vast steppe, it is always full of wonders. The house of Love (once also called the house of God) has roofs and doors made of *ghazals* and songs, and perhaps one may find the moonlike beloved on its roof. It can be a monastery, just as it can be the cave in which the Prophet and his faithful friend Abu Bakr spent the night of their emigration "as two names and one soul," hidden from the eyes of the world, for Love unites lover and beloved into a single being. In many of Rumi's verses the powerful, often even the cruel side of Love prevails. The separation from Shams, and perhaps some subconscious memory of his blood shed just beyond the doorstep, seem to surface in certain images. And Maulana knows from experience that there is no way out once Love has taken over the human heart,

> For Love has grasped my hem and drags it
> as a hungry man clutches the edge of the tablecloth. . . .
>
> (D 3073)

Therefore it is also impossible to conceal Love. It is as conspicuous as a camel on top of a minaret (D 1624).

Love often appears as a trap or a net for the soul-bird. What bird would flee from the grains, sugar, and almonds that are held out as bait?

> Someone who is far away from the net of Love
> Is a bird that does not have a wing!

For, as Maulana reminds us, only the lovely birds fall into Love's trap, not creatures like the owl, who refuses to look at the sun and is content to remain among the ruins. The paradox of Love is that the more one is captured by it, the freer one becomes. Only Love can enable one to fly heavenward, to tear the veils that separate lover from beloved. Therefore, even the Simurgh, the symbol of Divinity, does not return to his residence on Mount Qaf at the end of the world once he has fallen into Love's snare.

Love's strong hand spares no one; even lions tremble and are captured by it, and elephants become like helpless cats in Love's bag or else are pierced by the horn of the unicorn "Love" and carried away. One can become happy only when eagerly awaiting this cruel treatment, for it is the lover's dream to be sacrificed for and by the beloved. Love is the great feast of offerings, and the lover, who longs to be accepted as a sacrificial lamb, fears lest through suffering he may have become too skinny and no longer plump enough to be acceptable for the sacrifice. That would be disastrous, for spiritual growth is possible only through constant loving self-sacrifice.

However, it is not only during the great feast that Love slaughters the lover; Love is in general a man-eating monster. That is why Maulana urges the lover to become a true "man," *mard,* so that he will constitute a sweet morsel for Love.

Associations of Love with images of human heroism occur often: the whole road toward Love is filled with blood shed by Love's sword, and after dragging the poor intoxicated lover with a hook, Love eats his liver and finally devours him completely. Even more:

The whole world would become a morsel
If Love but had a mouth! (D 2435)

Love becomes fat from drinking the blood of the loving Muslims, and also makes the lover drink his own blood. Maulana's hope is:

To become blood, to drink one's own blood,
to sit with the dogs at the door of faithfulness. (D 2102)

The lover finally becomes blood in the veins of Love, tears in the lover's eyes, and thus reaches the highest possible station, the complete transformation into Love.

Sometimes Love appears as a cupper who bleeds the lover to purify him of his base qualities and make him spiritually healthier, but at other times Love is just nasty and may arrive in a state of intoxication to scratch the face of the person it has selected. Cruel and ever-hungry, Love can easily be a lion, triumphantly roaring in the forest of the soul and scaring away the flock of Grief:

Your love, a black lion, tears out all my bones!

Or it is a panther—not a tame cheetah, an animal who (as Rumi held, along with Sana'i) lives meekly on cheese. Just as readily as it can be the emerald that blinds dragons, it can be the dragon itself (a shifting of images that is very typical of Maulana's poetry), but more often it is a crocodile, and Sleep flees when he sees it just as a fish flees before an alligator. This crocodile can easily shatter the fragile boat "Intellect" in the ocean of Love. Then, in a more romantic trend, Love is the falcon that carries away the heart, which foolishly enough had laid a trap for the royal bird, not anticipating how strong it was! And despite its strength, Love is as radiant and beautiful as a peacock.

Not only animals serve Rumi in his attempts to tell his listeners all that Love is. It is a sultan, the prince of the fighters for the true faith. It can be the emperor of Byzans, Rum, who defeats spiritual laziness as though it were the army of the Ethiopians—an image that goes back to the medieval Alexander romance: Alexander overcame the Zanjis, the black armies, with ease. In the train of the victorious king, tears arrive like the little coins that are strewn about on festive occasions or during parades. For the emperor "Love" often goes marching with a huge army, and the souls are arrayed at the head, numerous as grains of sand, while the props of the soul-tents are of pure light. The warrior king and his army besiege the human heart and destroy the city of Intellect, or take prisoners. However, Love can also be the clarion player who plays the triumphant tune *Innā fataḥnā* (Sura 48/1), "Verily We have opened a victory."

The hero "Love" carries with him his sword (an Indian sword of good quality) and orders it to cut off the head of everything that exists besides him. Here, Maulana, like many other poets, plays on the word *la,* "no," the beginning of the profession of faith, *lā ilāha illā'Llāh* ("There is no deity save God"), in which the Arabic letters look almost like a two-edged sword. This sword, like 'Ali's Dhu'lfiqar, destroys everything other than the Divine Truth—or, as Rumi says, other than Love. Yet not everyone is worthy of being slain by the sword of Love, for

> Would the bloodthirsty lion drink the blood of dogs?

Sometimes Love is a shieldmaker to protect man; at other times a sultan with mighty bows and arrows (a symbol typical of mystical love poetry throughout the world), and the lover's heart and liver are pierced by the arrows.

> From arrows this liver is barbed like the back of a
> porcupine!
> If Love had a liver, it would have pity! (D 1067)

Like a true king, Love brandishes his flag to protect the lovers, or travels with hundreds of drums and flags. Amid this martial glory it can easily plunder the country "Heart," for like a true

Turkish hero, Love is used to *yaghmā,* plundering. Here as elsewhere, "Turk" is the designation for the powerful, radiant, and cruel beloved, the princely rider who can tame even the restive mustang "Heaven."

After such a destructive attack, when Love finally rules supreme (like Nushirwan, the Iranian paragon of justice), the inhabitants of the city will gladly offer their lives to him, like Hatim, the ancient Arabic model of generosity.

> How happy is the town whose king Love is!
> There every street is feasting, every house a festivity,

and the human being, or his soul, will gladly become Love's servant or maid.

The personification of Love as a ruler is not unheard of, but there are other images in Maulana's work that verge on the grotesque. Who else would see Love as the police officer, *shiḥna,* who goes to the town to demand confiscation from every living creature, which means that he applies all kinds of torture? However, the poem with the recurrent rhyme *muṣādara,* "confiscation" (D 2288), speaks also of the winter as confiscating the belongings of the trees, but these are recompensed in spring by the sun's kindness. The implication is that those whose belongings have been confiscated by Love will receive something even more precious in return.

As a police officer, Love can also open the door of the prison—that is, of this world—for it has a great bunch of keys under its arm (D 2236); in one passage Maulana asks it to make a key whose teeth consist of the word "Joy" (D 2918).

The police officer also has instruments to brand the lover like an animal that is branded by its owner (however, after receiving this mark, he will be exempt from paying taxes). In a related image, Love appears as the judge who extorts taxes, but since the village "Heart" is completely ruined, how is the poor lover to pay? This idea in turn leads to an image of Love as a highwayman before whom all are stripped of their clothes, or else it is simply a thief who steals everything from the house, or a cutpurse:

> Love cut off my purse. I said: "What are you doing?"
> It said: "Is not my boundless grace enough for you?" (D 1830)

For one who has entered the path of Love no longer needs any of the colorful things of this world. Even more bizarre is Rumi's image of Love in the guise of a ragman, calling out in Turkish, *Eski babuç kimde var,* "Who has got old shoes?" to ensure that nothing may be left to remind the lover of the outward, transient world of matter. And the poet dramatically describes how his personified Love for Shams runs about everywhere, its eyes filled with blood and a sword in its hand, searching for the lover's soul while other people are fast asleep, so that finally the lover's "vessel fell from the roof" (i.e., his secret was revealed) and everyone in town realized that some mysterious burglary had taken place.

Love is a washerman who breaks the fragile bleach bottle "Repentance" by his rough treatment, or it itself is a bottlemaker who fashions the bottle of the Heart. More logically, it appears as a carpenter who builds the ladder that leads to heaven, if Rumi does not see it as the ladder itself.

Maulana's love of food imagery emerges again where he sees Love invite its guests to dine on the dry and wet food, which is procured by the lover's dry lips and wet eyes, or it simply places a flaming table before its guest. The heart becomes an iron pot on the fire of Love, but Love is also personified as the great baker thanks to whom the raw is cooked. Images of this kind occur frequently, and the Sufi usage of the term *dhauq,* "tasting," to refer to immediate experience may have contributed to this imagery. Love itself can even constitute the nourishment of the lovers; they "eat Love." And if sugar knew how sweet Love is, it would dissolve to water in its shame. . . . Some of Maulana's descriptions of Love as the great cook who prepares the *tutmaj,* a kind of vermicelli, for the lovers are so paradoxical that one can barely untangle them.

Yet if Love is a cook, it can also be a weaver or tailor, for it stitches things together without thread and needle. Rumi is not clear as to whether the person whom Love has denuded will or will not be given a new garment, but he states that Love is indeed the robe of honor for the soul. He knows well that whatever is woven in Love's factory without the beloved will not last, for warp and woof fall apart.

Love next appears as the great sorcerer who seizes the lover's ear to cast a spell over him in a secret corner. But it boasts more respectable professions as well. Often it acts as a physician and is then interchangeable with the beloved. To be sure, it is sometimes called Galen, but how can Galen or Plato compare with the eternal wise physician who both confers and heals the heart's ailment and who offers it a *mufarriḥ,* a kind of tranquilizer? When Rumi holds a dialogue with Dr. Love, this physician prescribes a diet and gives the ill person a drink so that "you may not come to yourself until eternity." As Love can be the physician, it can also be the *imām* whose presence fills a thousand mosques.

It is natural that Love should be represented as one of the Koranic prophets, and here it is usually Moses, with his miraculous wand turned into a powerful serpent: in other words, the dry human body can turn into a mighty serpent once Love takes it in its hand. Love is also like Ibrahim, before whom the lover is willing to be sacrificed like Ishmael. It is the beautiful Yusuf, and it is Jesus with his life-bestowing breath, just as it is Solomon whose magic seal subdues *djinns* and who understands the language of the birds, the secret words of the heart. Love is David, in whose hand iron becomes pliable and who can soften even an iron heart. But it is also the highest manifestation of the long line of prophets, the Prophet Muhammad, the perfect manifestation of Divine Love: "Love comes like Mustafa in the midst of the infidels."

As much as Love is cruel and overpowering, yet it can also appear as a feminine power, for it is the mother who gives birth to humankind as well as to the four elements. Love is indeed the preeternal Mary, pregnant by the Divine Spirit, a mother who looks after her children tenderly (in contrast to the harlot "World," who devours her offspring). Who would not suck the teats of Love? Fleeing the depravity of mundane life, the human heart cuddles at Love's bosom—expressions that remind the reader of Baha'-i Walad's descriptions of the loving embrace of God. Love is everything, wetnurse and father, maternal uncle and paternal uncle. Is it not Love who, though itself without form and hands, gives each human being form and hands by uniting father and mother in the love game?

However, such soft words are rare, for Love (as Maulana never tired of saying) is meant only for the strong, and it is impossible to enjoy a comfortable life once Love has taken hold of one's heart. Timid little Sleep has to suffer terribly under Love's fists and finally runs away from the lover to join someone else's bed. For Love thrashes everything; it crushes stones and pounds them so that they may yield antimony, which enhances the eyesight. It also turns all cheeks to gold. Alchemical imagery is frequently used because it expresses the mystic's goal, the transformation of base matter into gold. But even if it were not the great alchemy that changes all for the better, as Maulana repeats still in the last section of the *Mathnawī*, it is a treasure that can be found only in ruins, the Divine Treasure of which God says, *Kuntu kanzan makhfiyyan,* "I was a hidden treasure and wanted to be known." Such treasure can be found only in the heart that is broken for Love's, or God's, sake. The great miracle of Love is that it always carries the lover to higher stages: once the lower soul, the *nafs,* has been touched by Love, it can no longer become *ammāra,* "that which instigates to evil" (Sura 12/53), just as the hideous demon who falls in love can ultimately occupy a higher place than Gabriel himself.

Love is wine and cupbearer alike, and its drink is poison and antidote at the same time. It is a heady wine, to be sure, and intoxicates humankind unto eternity. As a result of such fiery wine, "each one feels so hot that his coat seems too tight and he takes off his cap and opens his belt"—a very drastic description of what German mystics called *Gottesfülle* ("being completely filled with God"). The lovers are filled with the wine of Love; rather, they even appear to be the very bottle or the goblet of Love.

> God has created me from the wine of Love!

Thus thinks Maulana, and he admonishes his reader to remember that sober people are disgraced before the assembly of Love. But what of *'aql,* "reason," "intellect," which is such an important part of our being and whose duty it is to guide its owner on the right path, to check his passions?

> Love became plump and fat and handsome,
> Reason turned toward leanness. (D 2190)

Thus says Maulana in a line that reminds the modern reader of John Donne's remark about love's "cumbersome unwieldiness." The lover has become all too skinny under the influence of Love, and yet

> The moon's leanness comes from its proximity to the sun.
>
> (D 2942)

The farther the moon is from the sun, the more it waxes and becomes fat—but that, as Maulana teaches us, is no honor, for why would one want to live far from the sun, from Shams? And Intellect behaves in exactly the same way: it wanes once Love comes. How can the proud camel "Love" be squeezed into the little den built for the chicken "Intellect"?

> If for your chicken you have built a den,
> A camel will not fit there, it's too large!
> The den: your body, and the chicken: reason;
> Love is the camel, glorious and high! (D 2937)

Could Abu Hanifa and Shafi'i, founders of two of the schools of Islamic law, have any idea what Love is? asks Rumi, taking over this question from Sana'i. For reason may know all about religious duties and legal prescriptions, but it knows nothing of the religious school of Love.

> Those with intellect run away from a dead ant out of
>   caution;
> Lovers trample heedlessly on dragons! (D 2366)

For reason, or intellect, contemplates the last consequences of every act, while Love flies to heaven with no care for the results, leaving science and etiquette to Intellect. It is an idea that is echoed in the poetry of Muhammad Iqbal, who in this respect is a loyal follower of Rumi.

While Intellect is happy to nibble dainties, *nuql,* from the inherited sciences, *naql,* Love is vision; Intellect sees only the world of matter and believes that the six directions are the limit, while Love knows the way into the realm of the limitless and owns, hidden behind the veils of blood, a rose garden. Rumi reminds his reader of Hallaj, who "gave up the pulpit for the gallows," for only by becoming a martyr, *shahīd,* of Love can one become a witness, *shāhid,* and give public testimony to Love's power—which is impossible for the law-bound preacher on the pulpit who is constrained to discuss religious duties. Like Hallaj, the lover knows that once Love has slain him, Love itself, or its beauty, will be the blood money to recompense him. Intellect is the *qādī,* the judge; but once Love appears he loses his turban, the sign of his position; nay, he may even pawn it for the goblet of Love! And strange goings-on are reported when Love arrives in town:

> Prison became Paradise through the clamor of Love:
> Mr. Justice Intellect, drunk on the judge's bench!
> They came to Professor Reason to ask:
> "Why has this terrible riot happened in Islam?"

Mufti First Intellect answered with a *fatwā* [legal decision]:
"This is the moment of resurrection—where is [the
    difference between] licit and illicit?"
The preacher "Love" came to the *'īdgāh* [place of prayer] of
    Union
With the sword Dhu'lfiqar and said: "Praise that king
Who strews forth from the ocean of Nowhere
Jewel-like souls. . . ." (D 202)

Intellect may be a Plato in his own right, but:

> Love took up a mace and beat Intellect's head.

Even worse, when Sultan Love arrives, he removes King Intellect
from his throne and hangs him on the gallows like a thief.
Therefore, Intellect flees from house to house when he sees Love
appear in the guise of Prince Bloodshedding.

Yet there is some hope that Intellect may one day participate in
Love's activities—though usually he retreats to a corner like a
good ascetic when Love brings forth wine and roast. If he samples
a single grain from Love's bait, at once he loses his fine plumage,
or crawls meekly in the dust of Love's vestibule. He may even taste
some opium from Love's hand (D 1931) and become demented.
Then, when one wonders what has happened to him, he has a
good answer:

> I asked: "Dear Intellect, where are you?"
> And Intellect replied:
> "Since I've turned into wine, why should I
>   become a sour grape?" (D 2924)

This has at least some logic to it, for nothing that has been
changed for the better can return to its previous state. Even
stranger things may happen:

> Every morning out of love for you this Intellect becomes
>   crazy,

Climbs upon the roof of the brains and plays the lute. . . .

(D 2601)

It is natural for Maulana to extol Majnun, the demented lover, who sees his beloved Layla everywhere; for to surrender to Love means to give up one's normal life and traditional values, and thus to relinquish etiquette and shame.

Yet Love can transform even the most despicable creature into something valuable:

A loving dog is better than a sober lion!
The lion of the sky [the sign Leo] kisses his paw with that
lip which does not touch carrion. (D 1174)

Maulana continued to follow the injunctions of the religious law in his personal life, but he knew that love is beyond the hedge of letters. Will the lover spend time reading a love letter in the presence of the beloved? Certainly not, as Rumi tells in the *Mathnawī*. And no one has ever plucked a rose *(gul)* from the letters *g-l,* or has learned Love by spelling it out. And just as Love is beyond letters and rational knowledge, it transcends all religious rites:

Love entered the mosque and said: "O master and guide,
Tear off the shackles of existence—why are you still in the
fetters of the prayer rug?

Or, as Rumi puts it elsewhere:

Love is free from the narrowness of prayer niche and cross.

(D 355)

For Love is divine, and its voice calls human beings to return to their eternal home, to the realm of Divine Light, led by Muhammad Mustafa. In light of this quality, Love can be described as *mi'rāj,* a heavenly journey comparable to that of the Prophet, but also as Buraq, the mysterious steed that carried the Prophet into the Divine Presence; to know Love means to fly heavenward, and how can the soul-bird not use his wings to fly toward Love?

> When there is no foot, the lover flies with the wing of
> preeternity;
> When there is no head—the lover has other heads! (D 594)

Finally, when the state of *bīkhudī,* complete selflessness, is reached, Maulana sings of his confusion in a lovely dialogue with his beloved, or perhaps the dialogue is with Love itself:

> You ask me: "How are you?"
> > How can I know it?
> "From where? Which family?"
> > How can I know it?
> You ask me: "You are drunk,
> > intoxicated—
> From which sweet, heavy wine?"
> > How can I know it?
> If I myself am you,
> > Well, who are you, then?
> Are you this, are you that?
> > How can I know it?
>
> > (D 1544)

Whatever variegated imagery Rumi may use to "describe" Love, the images share a single common denominator: always the activity described begins from the side of Love, from the Divine Source: it is the falcon that carries away its prey, the fierce lion, the torrent, the king who besieges the city, the musician and the cupbearer, the devouring fire and the loving mother. Entrusting himself completely to this Divine Power, Maulana experiences the love of God enclosed in the fragile vessel of the heart:

> O Love that is too bulky to fit in the sky—
> How is it that you fit within my veiled heart?
> You leapt into the house of the heart and closed the door
> from inside,
> My niche and my glass and my "light upon Light" (Sura 24/
> 35) (D 1460)

Illuminated by this light, the lover recognizes that everything points to Divine Beauty and Majesty which, however, can never be attained by the human eye or thought, because the jealousy of Love hides its essence behind roses and nightingales. In Love, the two Divine Names *al-mumit,* "He who kills," and *al-Muḥyī,* "He who bestows life," manifest themselves:

> He who has become Love's prey,
> how can he become the prey of death?

Azra'il, the angel of death, has no hold upon lovers, because the lover is killed by the sword of Love, yet resurrected through the trumpet of Love, and, as Maulana says:

> Lovers are strange—the more they are killed, the more they
> are alive! (D 1075)

The mystery of rejuvenating death that lies behind the parable of the moth who casts itself into the flame to "become flame"— this is what Maulana experienced in his own life and what inspired the ritual of the whirling dance, in which death and resurrection in the orbit of the spiritual sun are symbolized in visible form:

> Those who know the secret power
> of the whirling, live in God:
> Love is slaying and reviving
> them—they know it. . . . *Allāh Hū!*

ﺭﯨﺴﻮ 11

They Enter All the Dance,
the Dance . . .

IT WAS IN DECEMBER 1954 that I received an invitation to partici-
pate in the celebration of Maulana's *shab-i 'arūs,* or "spiritual
nuptials," as the memorial day for a saint's death is called. I had
recently arrived in Ankara to teach there at the Faculty of Islamic
Theology, and had by that time published a number of German
verse translations of and smaller studies on Maulana's poetry.
Excited by the prospect of attending the first celebration of
Maulana's anniversary, I saw whirling dervishes in my dream, and
in the middle of the month happily set out with my mother for
Konya. We stayed with an amiable and well-to-do family, and late
in the evening we were brought to a large mansion in the center
of the old town, in which two armchairs had been set out for the
noble guests. With amazement we observed as a group of elderly
gentlemen unwrapped mysterious parcels out of which emerged
flutes, rebabs, tambourines, even dervish caps and gowns. What
was going on? The Mevlevi ritual had been prohibited ever since
Ataturk had closed the dervish lodges in 1925—how could it be
possible that all the implements were still in use? Hafiz Sabri, who
taught the recitation of the Koran in our faculty, smiled: "You'll
see, your dream will come true!"—and he was right. For the first
time in twenty-nine years the men began to perform the mystical

dance together, and we listened to the music, the flutes, the drums, the powerful introductory praise song for the Prophet, and saw the men turning, whirling, their white gowns unfolding as though they were large white moths turning around a candle or atoms whirling around the sun, like the stars in cosmic harmony. They had not practiced together for decades, but here they had gathered from Istanbul and Afyonkarahisar, from Samsun and from Ankara, and at once they found their way back to the old rhythm of the *samā'-i samāwī,* the "heavenly dance."

These Mevlevis performed the ritual as well during the official celebrations that took place over the following days, and on the final day they were permitted to perform it at the Yeşil Türbe, because it was planned to film the *samā'* in its traditional place. The film, however, was inexplicably destroyed in an accident, and only a few photographs remain.

In later years, the *samā'* became part and parcel of the annual celebrations held each December in Konya, and still later the Mevlevis periodically went on tour in various countries. Even those who do not know the religious background of the ritual are usually deeply impressed; but for me there was a slight change in the spirit of the dance once most of the old Mevlevis had passed away, for I could never forget that dreamlike night in Konya when everything was absolutely perfect. . . .

Not in vain are the Mevlevis known as Whirling Dervishes. But the *samā' (sema),* the music that is accompanied by whirling, was not invented by Maulana. In fact, the Sufis had begun to hold musical sessions as early as the second half of the ninth century, when the first hall for *samā'* was founded in Baghdad. Listening to music and the ensuing indulgence in ecstatic dance soon became a feature of Sufism that aroused much criticism from orthodox Muslims and even from members of the so-called "sober" fraternities, who were averse to music and in general to showing their rapture by outward sounds and movements. Many authors rightly reproached those for whom the word "Sufism" meant little else than listening to music and dancing. However, in no other Sufi order has the whirling movement been organized and institutionalized as in the Mevlevi order, where it is a carefully elaborated ritual that leaves no room for "ecstatic" movement but is built upon perfect harmony, with each movement having a special meaning.

The central place of the *samā'* in the Mevlevi order is understandable, as Maulana's poetry is largely born out of the sound of music and the whirling dance, which often continued for hours. When listening to his verses, especially the early lyrical pieces, one is often tempted to scan them according to the rhythm of an imaginary drum or tambourine, for the classical meters that he always applied were changed in his mouth and became, in many cases, more singable, more ecstatic.

Perhaps the most beautiful expression of Maulana's love of music is the introductory section of the *Mathnawī,* the "Song of the Reed":

> Oh hear the reed flute, how it does complain
> and how it tells of separation's pain. . . .

The flute, cut from its reed bed, cries out in loneliness and expresses its longing for home: thus it divulges to the world the secrets of primordial unity and eternal love. Living in Anatolia as he did, it is not surprising that Maulana was so fond of music: there the Phrygian flute had been known from ancient times, when early music theorists wrote of its complaining sounds, and ancient as well as medieval Islamic medicine was well aware of the healing and soothing powers of music: during Maulana's lifetime, a marvelous hospital was erected in Divrigi, far to the northeast of Konya, where an artfully arranged watercourse in a basin served to soothe the insane and melancholy inmates of the hospital. Similar institutions were known throughout medieval Islam.

As for the reed flute, however, its story too has roots in antiquity. King Midas of Gordion (situated not too far from Konya) was cursed by Apollo, so legend tells, with a pair of ass's ears. Hiding the ears under his Phrygian cap, he finally entrusted this terrible problem to his minister under the condition that the latter would never speak of it to anyone. After some time, however, the minister was no longer able to keep the secret and told it to a lake, where, he thought, it would be well kept. But a reed was growing on the bank of the lake, and when a shepherd cut the reed to make a flute, the flute began to tell the king's secret to the world. Islamic tradition has transformed this story: in Sana'i's *Ḥadīqa* it is the Prophet who entrusts the deepest mysteries of the faith to his cousin and son-in-law 'Ali, who like King Midas's minister tells them one day to a lake. Maulana even alludes to this tradition:

Like 'Ali I breathe into the depth of the well. (D 2380)

The flute offered itself as the instrument that best represents the human being, all the more as its sound is closest to that of the human voice. Furthermore, Maulana, along with other poets, could propose any number of associations between the reed flute and the reed pen: both are cut off from their home, both are trimmed by the friend's hand, and both reveal the secret of longing and love, the one in sweet melodies, and the other in beautiful letters, comparable in their movement to undulating melodies. A third aspect can easily be added: the reed is related to sugarcane, and both reed flute and reed pen are filled with sugar once the beloved handles them.

Maulana's poetry is replete with allusions to the *ney,* the reed flute. And was he himself not like a flute in the hands of his beloved? Could he have written a single line unless "this friend, this Turk" had "blown into him" and sung through his mouth?

The lovers, complaining like the reed flute, and Love like
the flute player—
What kinds of things does this Love breathe into the clarion
Body? (D 1936)

In the reed flute Maulana found the ideal metaphor for himself, his loving songs, and his endless longing for the eternal home, the reed bed of God's depths. He could refer, in this connection, to a word ascribed to the Prophet, who compared the believer to a *mizmār*, a wind instrument (D 1173) moved by God's breath. But in order to sing, the flute must be empty: hence the importance of fasting and abstinence.

Not only the flute offers itself to such comparisons (although it is ideal, thanks to its association with the breath that God breathed into Adam, as told in Sura 15/29); any instrument can similarly become a metaphor for the human being in the hand of the beloved.

> When your Love acts as musician, then I am
> Now a harp and now a viol, day and night! (D 302)

Is the lover not like a little harp, *chang,* in the "lap of your grace," bent toward the beloved's breast, singing when the friend's fingers touch him? And "the harp begins to lament under the fist of separation from you," as Rumi says with a pun on *chang,* which means both "harp" and "fist" (D 3088). The lover can appear as the *rabāb,* the small string instrument whose sound is such an essential part of Mevlevi music: his veins are like the strings of the *rabāb,* and the beloved uses the plectrum to produce sounds from him; only then can he respond with a sweet tune or a lamenting one. He may also be like the *barbaṭ,* the large lutelike instrument that is lazy and does not want to sing (D 1173); by "twisting its ear" one can properly tune it. However, the lover may also be a drum who begs the beloved not to beat it so heavily that it must suffer or its skin be torn. There is no end to such comparisons in Maulana's poetry, and like other poets he likes to play upon musical terminology: the term *parda,* meaning "veil" and "musical mode," appears in the very first verses of the *Mathnawī,* where he states that the reed flute's musical modes *(parda)* have torn the veils *(parda)* that hide Reality from human eyes. The technical names given to forms of melodical sequence, such as *Ḥijāz, 'Irāq, Rāst* ("correct"), or *'Ushshāq* (lit., "lovers"), can be used to create deliberately ambiguous lines in which he combines the primary and secondary meaning.

Maulana's love for music is related in numerous anecdotes. Once, it is told, on entering his room he found his disciples discussing Ibn 'Arabi's great mystical opus, the *Futūḥāt al-makkiyya,* ("The Meccan Openings"). He listened for a moment; then Abu Bakr the *rabāb* player entered and began to play. Maulana smiled, "Are not the *futūḥāt* [openings] of Abu Bakr-i *rabābī* better than the *Futūḥāt al-makkiyya?*" The immediate experience of the Divine through the sound of music was closer to his heart than the highly sophisticated work of the great master Ibn 'Arabi, whose approach to the Divine can be found too theoretical and—according to Shamsuddin's criticism of Ibn 'Arabi's thought—too self-centered. Better to lose oneself in the fire of love that consumes everything, including logical and metaphysical thought!

The story may or may not be true—I believe it has a ring of truth to it—but another anecdote expresses the master's feeling about music even more succinctly. He once said to his visitors, "Music is the creaking of the doors of Paradise." A sober, critical, and according to Maulana rather unpleasant man responded, "But I don't like the creaking of doors!" Whereupon Maulana said, "I hear the doors as they open; as for you, you hear them when they close!"

The *samā',* the mystical dance, opens the gates to Paradise. Therefore it is one of the most important aspects—one may even say, the axis—of Maulana's poetry. His friends, including his female disciples, would arrange *samā'* parties for him, and the secret power behind the *samā'* was the presence, in body or spirit, of the beloved. The very name of Shams causes "even the dead . . . to dance in their shrouds": *samā'* prefigures resurrection and Paradise. The poems, anecdotes, and legends also make clear how important the presence of Husamuddin Chelebi was for Maulana in later years, and how sharply the poet reacted if he was disturbed in his dance by impolite behavior.

Samā' appears in Rumi's poetry in the guise of various images. It is the ladder to heaven, a ladder the longing soul can climb to reach the roof where the radiant, beautiful Beloved will be waiting. But *samā'* is much more than a time-bound ritual movement, for the entire universe is busy with dancing, whirling, stamping its feet—indeed, the number of poems with the recurrent rhyme *pā kūfta,* "have stamped their feet," and similar expressions speaks for itself. Maulana sees the bees dancing in the delight of *samā',* and the Beloved's glory is so great that a hundred manifestations of divine glory *(kibriya)* stamp their feet. The flowers are stamping their feet over the tomb of January, their cruel enemy, and the trees likewise dance in the spring breeze. To stamp one's feet on the ground means to bring forth the Water of Life, which will gush forth when dancers' feet touch the ground, and the call of Love's melody, singing out the Beloved's name, resurrects the dead. Now the flowers enter the dance before the nightingale, their music master, and the stars dance around the sun or around the heavenly pole. Even more:

> Gabriel dances for love of the beauty of God,
> The vile demon, *'ifrīt,* dances too for love of a she-demon!
>
> (D 2763)

It is not surprising that angels and demons alike have joined the whirling, for Maulana sees everything clapping its hands and dancing:

> Hand-clapping, the Universal Reason,
> Dancing, parts and the Whole.

Even creation itself is described as the ecstatic dance of those future beings who, longing for existentialization while still in *'adam,* Not-Being, hear the Divine Address and run out into the worlds of Existence to take up the intoxicated whirling and then manifest themselves as flowers and trees (D 1832). Now each one rushes like a torrent toward the ocean that is its source, and, as Maulana continues with a pun on *kaf* ("foam" and "hand"), "foaming, or clapping our hands, we go there" (D 1713): thus the way back to the beginning is also a dance.

Likewise, the individual heart begins to dance when the beloved looks at it:

> When Shams-i Tabriz but looks at the Koran copy "Heart,"
> The case endings dance, the reading signs stamp their feet
>
> (D 2282)

The theme of *samā'* occurs less frequently in the *Mathnawī,* except for references in a few stories, such as the one above the Sufi who sought shelter in a Sufi residence where the brethren, hoping to procure money for a merry *samā'* party, sold his donkey without his knowledge. But the majority of the poems about and allusions to the dance are, understandably, found in the *Dīwān,* many of whose quatrains served the musicians as new texts and were "born" in the movement of the dance.

Most religious traditions have viewed dance as a way to relinquish one's earth-bound gravity and become united with the spiritual world; whether one thinks of the wild Dionysian revels or the harmonious Apollonian dance of classical antiquity, whether one considers the Native American sun and rain dances, or the cultic dances to honor the deities as was common in the tradition of India, dance is always something that leads us out of this world of matter. Maulana knew this well, and his love for the spiritual Sun Shamsuddin is aptly expressed in the language of dance.

As for the well-regulated ritual of the Mevlevis, it has been interpreted in various ways. It may be that the dervishes, turning around their own axis and at the same time around the master, represent the dust specks or atoms that move around the sun, attracted and unified by the gravitational force of that central luminary that gathers them into a single movement, one that is entirely dependent on the sun's power.

One can also see in the *samā'* the movement of the spheres around the pole, the heavenly dance that permeates all of creation from the angels down to the least minerals. But one can also interpret it as a dance of death and resurrection: the dervishes, solemn in their long black cloaks, walk thrice around the *meydan,* the place where the master stands, to kiss his hands. Then, as the character of the music changes, they cast off their black cloaks, symbols of the perishable earthly body, and emerge in their white gowns, symbols of the spiritual body, the transfigured person at the time of resurrection. Next, they whirl around the spiritual center, moths dancing around the candle: the *sama'* is a symbol of death and resurrection in Love, an ever-newly enacted return to the Fountain of Life. Beginning with the hymn in honor of the Prophet, whose closest confidant Shams-i Tabriz is, it ends with a long, sonorous prayer and the deep call *Hū!* ("He!"), the acknowledgment that He is the One who gives life and death; who is the Living from whom everything comes and to whom everything will return.

Therefore Maulana calls us, as he has called his friends for seven centuries, to participate in the dance that moves through the universe, to circle around the Sun of Love:

> Oh come, oh come! You are the soul
> > of the soul of the soul of whirling!
> Oh come! You are the cypress tall
> > in the blooming garden of whirling!
> Oh come! For there has never been
> > and will never be one like you!
> Come, one like you have never seen
> > the longing eyes of whirling!
> Oh come! The fountain of the sun
> > is hidden under your shadow!

You own a thousand Venus stars
    in the circling heavens of whirling!
The whirling sings your praise and thanks
    with a hundred eloquent tongues:
I'll try to say just one, two points
    translating the language of whirling.
For when you enter in the dance
    you then leave both these worlds
For outside these two worlds there lies
    the universe, endless, of whirling.
The roof is high, the lofty roof
    that is on the seventh sphere,
But far beyond this roof is raised
    the ladder, the ladder of whirling.
Whatever there is, is only He,
    your foot steps there in dancing:
The whirling, see, belongs to you,
    and you belong to the whirling.
What can I do when Love appears
    and puts its claw round my neck?
I grasp it, take it to my breast
    and drag it into the whirling!
And when the bosom of the motes
    is filled with the glow of the sun,
They enter all the dance, the dance
    and do not complain in the whirling!

 Bibliography

WORKS BY RUMI

Citations of the *Dīwān-i kabīr* are noted in the text with the letter D and the number of the poem. Citations of *Mathnawī-yi ma'nawī* are noted with the letter M and the number of the book (in Roman numerals) and the line. Translations of the *Mathnawī* exist in all Oriental languages (Arabic, Turkish, Urdu, Sindhi, Panjabi, in part in Bengali and Pashto); selections from Rumi's work are available in all European languages, especially German.

Dīwān-i kabīr, ed. Badī'uzzamān Furūzānfar. 10 vols. Tehran: University of Tehran, 1957–1976.

Fīhi mā fīhi, ed. Badī'uzzamān Furūzānfar. Tehran: Amir Kabir, 1348 SH/1969. Translated by Arthur J. Arberry as *Discourses of Rumi.* London: John Murray, 1961. German: *Von Allem und vom Einen,* trans. Annemarie Schimmel. Munich: Diederichs, 1988.

Mathnawī-yi ma'nawī, ed. Reynold A. Nicholson, with translation and commentary. 8 vols. London: Luzac, 1925–1940.

Maktūbāt, ed. Faridun Nafiz Uzluk. Istanbul: Sebat, 1937.

Selected Poems from the Dīwān-i Shams-i Tabrīz, trans. and ed. Reynold A. Nicholson. Cambridge: Cambridge University Press, 1898, repr. 1961. An excellent selection.

OTHER WORKS

Aflāki, Shamsuddīn. *Manāqib al-'ārifīn,* ed. Tahsin Yazīcī. 2 vols. Ankara: Türk Tarih Kurumu, 1959–1961.

Arberry, Arthur J. *The Rubā'iyyāt of Jalāl al-Dīn Rūmī.* London: E. Walker, 1949.

———. *Tales from the Masnavi.* London: George Allen and Unwin, 1961.

———. *More Tales from the Masnavi.* London: George Allen and Unwin, 1968.

———. *Mystical Poems of Rumi: First Selection,* poems 1–200. Chicago: University of Chicago Press, 1968. *Second Selection,* poems 201–400. Boulder, Colo.: Westview Press, 1979.

Bahā'uddīn Walad. *Ma'ārif,* ed. Badī'uzzamān Furūzānfar. 2nd ed. Tehran, 1353 SH/1974.

Chelkowski, Peter J., ed. *The Scholar and the Saint.* New York: New York University Press, 1975.

Chittick, William C. *The Sufi Path of Love.* Albany: SUNY Press, 1983.

Friedlander, Shams. *The Whirling Dervishes.* New York: 1975, 1991.

Gölpĭnarli, Abdulbaki. *Mevlâna Celâladdin. Hayatĭ, felsefesi, eserlerinden seçmeler.* Istanbul: Varlĭk, 1952.

Hastie, William. *The Festival of Spring from the Dîvân of Jalâl ed-Dîn.* Glasgow: James MacLehose & Sons, 1903.

Iqbal, Afzal. *The Life and Work of Muhammad Jalal ud-Din Rumi.* 3rd ed. Lahore: Institute of Islamic Culture, 1974.

Khalifa Abdul Hakim. *The Metaphysics of Rumi.* Lahore: Ashraf, 1933, 1948.

Meier, Fritz. *Bahā'-i Walad.* Acta Iranica 27. Leiden: Brill, 1989.

Molé, Marijan. *La Danse extatique en Islam.* Sources Orientales vi. Paris: Editions du Seuil, 1963.

Nicholson, Reynold Alleyne. *Rumi: Poet and Mystic.* London: George Allen and Unwin, 1950.

Önder, Mehmet. *Mevlâna bibliografyasi:1 Basmalar; 2 Yazmalar.* Ankara: Iş Bankasĭ, 1973, 1975.

Ritter, Hellmut. "Maulānā Ǧalāluddīn Rūmī und sein Kreis: Philologika XI." *Der Islam* 26 (1942): 116–158, 221–249.

―――. "Die Mevlânafeier in Konya vom 11–17 Dezember 1960." *Oriens* 15 (1962): 249–270.

Sabagh, Georges, ed. *The Heritage of Rumi: Proceedings of the Eleventh Levi della Vida Conference.* Cambridge: Cambridge University Press, forthcoming.

Schimmel, Annemarie. *The Triumphal Sun: A Study of the Life and Works of Mowlana Jalaloddin Rumi.* London & The Hague: East-West Publications, 1978, 1980.

―――. *As through a Veil: Mystical Poetry in Islam.* New York: Columbia University Press, 1982.

―――. *Mystical Dimensions of Islam.* Chapel Hill: University of North Carolina Press, 1975.

―――, ed. *Güldeste,* a collection of papers on Rumi. Konya, 1971.

Sipahsālār, Farīdūn. *Risāla dar aḥwāl-i Maulānā Jalāluddīn Rūmī,* ed. Badī 'uzzamān Furūzānfar. Tehran, 1325 SH/1946.

Sultan Walad. *Waladnāma,* ed. Jalāl Humā'ī. Tehran, 1315 SH/1936.

Whinfield, H. *Masnawi-i manawi: Spiritual Couplets* (1881). Translated and abridged. London: Octagon Press, 1973.

 Index

CONCEPTS AND TECHNICAL TERMS

KORANIC REFERENCES

BOOKS MENTIONED

Shambhala Dragon Editions

The Art of War, by Sun Tzu. Translated by Thomas Cleary.

The Awakened One: A Life of the Buddha, by Sherab Chödzin Kohn.

The Awakening of Zen, by D. T. Suzuki.

Bodhisattva of Compassion: The Mystical Tradition of Kuan Yin, by John Blofeld.

The Buddhist I-Ching. Translated by Thomas Cleary.

The Compass of Zen, by Zen Master Seung Sahn. Foreword by Stephen Mitchell.

The Dawn of Tantra, by Herbert V. Guenther and Chögyam Trungpa.

The Essence of Buddhism: An Introduction to Its Philosophy and Practice, by Traleg Kyabgon.

The Essential Teachings of Zen Master Hakuin: A Translation of the Sokko-roku Kaien-fusetsu, by Norman Waddell.

The Experience of Insight: A Simple and Direct Guide to Buddhist Meditation, by Joseph Goldstein.

The Five Houses of Zen, translated by Thomas Cleary.

A Flash of Lightning in the Dark of Night: A Guide to the Bodhisattva's Way of Life, by Tenzin Gyatso, the Fourteenth Dalai Lama.

Glimpses of Abhidharma, by Chögyam Trungpa.

Great Eastern Sun: The Wisdom of Shambhala, by Chögyam Trungpa.

The Heart of Awareness: A Translation of the Ashtavakra Gita, by Thomas Byrom

Kensho: The Heart of Zen, by Thomas Cleary.

Lieh-tzu: A Taoist Guide to Practical Living, by Eva Wong.

Living at the Source: Yoga Teachings of Vivekananda, by Swami Vivekananda.

Living with Kundalini: The Autobiography of Gopi Krishna, by Gopi Krishna.

Mastering the Art of War, by Zhuge Liang and Liu Ji. Translated and edited by Thomas Cleary.

The Mysticism of Sound and Music, by Hazrat Inayat Khan.

Nine-Headed Dragon River: Zen Journals 1969–1982, by Peter Matthiessen.

Returning to Silence: Zen Practice in Daily Life, by Dainin Katagiri. Foreword by Robert Thurman.

Rumi's World: The Life and Work of the Great Sufi Poet, by Annemarie Schimmel.

Shambhala: The Sacred Path of the Warrior, by Chögyam Trungpa.

The Shambhala Dictionary of Buddhism and Zen. Translated by Michael H. Kohn.

The Sutra of Hui-neng, Grand Master of Zen: With Hui-neng's Commentary on the Diamond Sutra. Translated by Thomas Cleary.

Vitality, Energy, Spirit: A Taoist Sourcebook. Translated and edited by Thomas Cleary.

Wen-tzu: Understanding the Mysteries, by Lao-tzu. Translated by Thomas Cleary.

The Wheel of Life: The Autobiography of a Western Buddhist, by John Blofeld.

Worldly Wisdom: Confucian Teachings of the Ming Dynasty, translated and edited by J. C. Cleary.

Zen Dawn: Early Zen Texts from Tun Huang, translated by J. C. Cleary.

Zen Essence: The Science of Freedom. Translated and edited by Thomas Cleary.